I0480158

ART BOOKS

FROM CRESCENT MOON PUBLISHING

Leonardo da Vinci
by James Pearson

Early Netherlandish Painting
by Rosalind Mutter

Piero della Francesca
by Naomi Haskell

Giovanni Bellini
by Julia Davis

Eric Gill: Nuptials of God
by Anthony Hoyland

Minimal Art and Artists In the 1960s and After
by Laura Garrard

Postwar Art
by George Knighton

Vincent van Gogh: Visionary Landscapes
by Stuart Morris

Max Beckmann
by Stuart Morris

Egon Schiele: Sex and Death in Purple Stockings
by D. Simon Eade

Mark Rothko: The Art of Transcendence
by Julia Davis

Jasper Johns
by L.M. Poole

Brice Marden
by Laura Garrard

Frank Stella: American Abstract Artist
by James Pearson

The Light Eternal: J.M.W. Turner
by Jeremy Mark Robinson

Maurice Sendak and the Art of Children's Book Illustration
by L.M. Poole

Sex in Art: Pornography and Pleasure in Painting and Sculpture
by Cassidy Hughes

Glorification: Religious Abstraction
In Renaissance and 20th Century Painting
by Jeremy Mark Robinson

The Art of Andy Goldsworthy
by William Malpas

Andy Goldsworthy: Touching Nature
by William Malpas

Andy Goldsworthy In Close-Up
by William Malpas

The Art of Richard Long
by William Malpas

Constantin Brancusi: Sculpting the Essence of Things
by James Pearson

Alison Wilding: The Embrace of Sculpture
by Susan Quinnell

The Erotic Object: Sexuality in Sculpture
From Prehistory to the Present Day
by Susan Quinnell

Land Art: A Complete Guide to Landscape, Environmental,
Earthworks, Nature, Sculpture and Installation Art
by William Malpas

Land Art In Close-Up
by William Malpas

Colourfield Painting: Minimal, Cool, Hard Edge, Serial
and Post-Painterly Abstract Art From the Sixties to the Present
by Laura Garrard

Bellini
By Jennie Ellis Keysor

The Life of Michelangelo Buonarroti
By John Addington Symonds

Dante Gabriel Rossetti
By Esther Wood

Rodin: The Man and His Art
Edited by Judith Cladel

Rodin
By Rainer Maria Rilke

Fra Angelico
By James Mason

The Madonna In Art
By Estelle Hurll

The Venetian School of Painting
By Evelyn Phillipps

Boucher
By Haldane McFall

Leonardo da Vinci
By Maurice Brockwell

Famous European Painters
By Sarah Bolton

Delacroix
By Paul Konody

Frederic Lord Leighton

Frederic Lord Leighton

An Illustrated Record of

His Life and Work

Ernest Rhys

CRESCENT MOON

First published 1900. This edition © 2018.

Printed and bound in the U.S.A.
Set in Book Antiqua 10 on 14pt.
Designed by Radiance Graphics.

Thanks to the authors and publishers quoted.

British Library Cataloguing in Publication data

ISBN-13 9781861716453

CRESCENT MOON PUBLISHING
P.O. Box 1312, Maidstone, Kent, ME14 5XU
Great Britain, www.crmoon.com

CONTENTS

NOTE ON THE TEXT

The text is from *Frederic Lord Leighton: An Illustrated Record of His Life and Works*, published by George Bell & Sons, London, 1900.

Footnotes are in square brackets, thus: [*1]

Lord Leighton, Self-Portrait, 1880, Uffizi Gallery

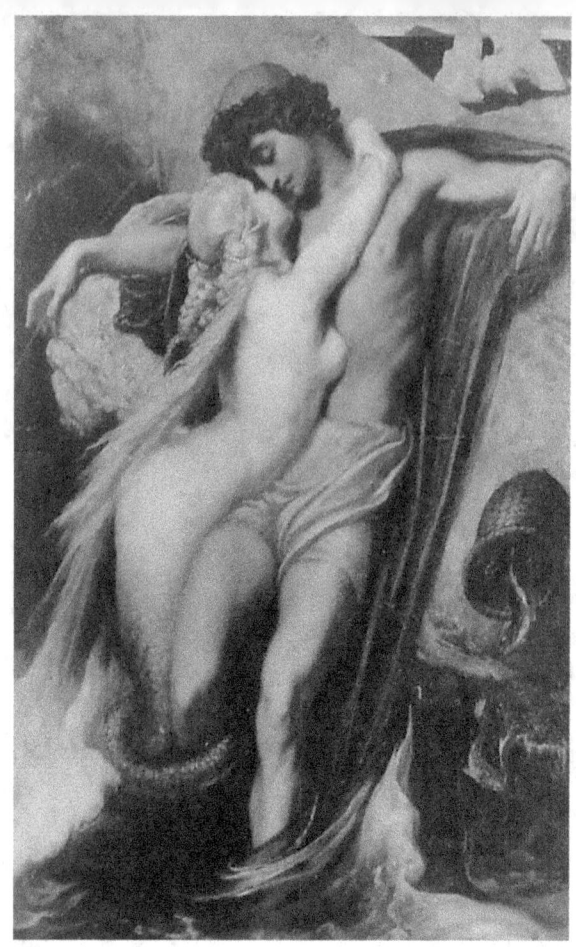

Classic Victorian nude imagery, by Lord Leighton: The Fisherman and the Siren, 1858, Bristol, above; and Actaea, the Nymph of the Shore, 1868, Ottawa, below.

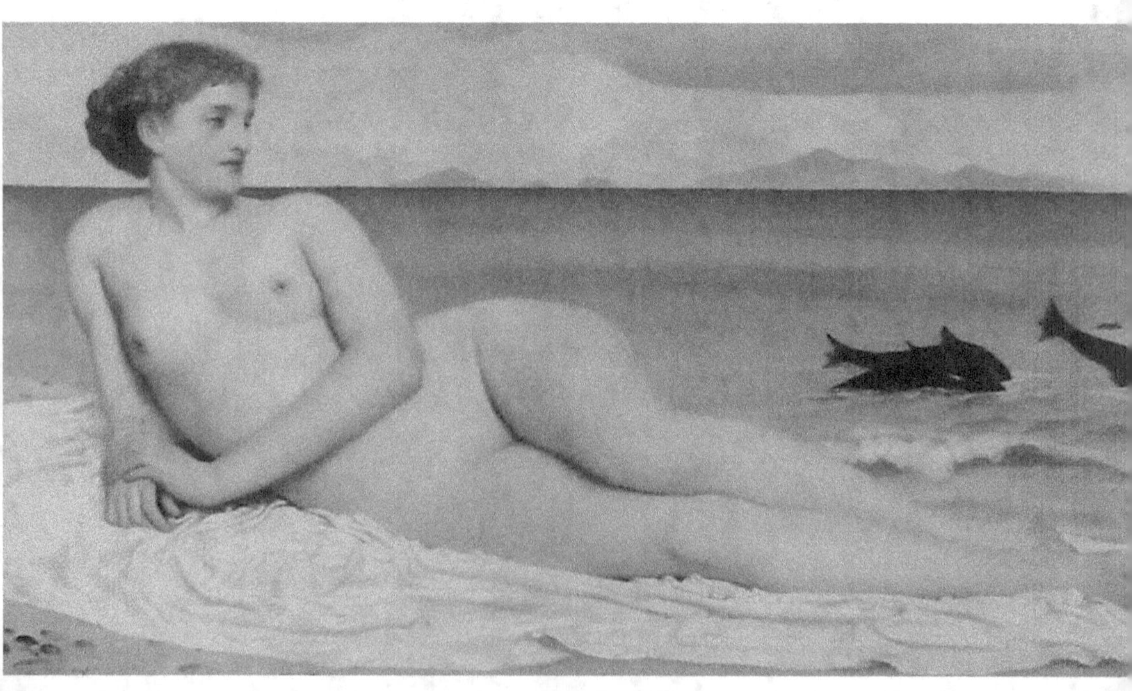

Publishers' Note to Third Edition

The reception given to previous editions of this work encourages the publishers to hope that a re-issue in a smaller form may be appreciated. The present volume is reprinted with a few alterations and corrections from the second edition published in 1898. A chapter on "Lord Leighton's House in 1900," by Mr. S. Pepys Cockerell, has been added.

The publishers take the opportunity to repeat their acknowledgments of assistance most kindly given by numerous owners and admirers of the artist's work. By the gracious consent of H.M. the Queen, the *Cimabue* in the Buckingham Palace collection, is here reproduced. Especial thanks are also due to Lord Davey, Lord Hillingdon, Lord Rosebery, Mrs. Dyson-Perrins, the late Mr. Alfred Morrison, Sir Bernhard Samuelson, Lady Hallé, Mr. Alex. Henderson, Mr. Francis Reckitts, the late Sir Henry Tate, the Birmingham and Manchester Corporations, and the President and Council of the Royal Academy, who have kindly permitted the reproduction of pictures in their possession. To the late Lord Leighton himself the author and publishers have to acknowledge their indebtedness for a large number of studies and sketches, hitherto unpublished, as well as for his kind co-operation in the preparation of the volume. The author wishes also to record his thanks to Mr. M. H. Spielmann for permission to use his admirable account of the President's method of painting.

By arrangement with the holders of several important copyrights, including Messrs. Thos. Agnew and Sons, P. and D. Colnaghi and Co., H. Graves and Co., Arthur Tooth and Sons, the Society for Promoting Christian Knowledge, the proprietors of the Art Journal, the Berlin Photographic Company, and the Fine Art Society (whose courtesies in the matter are duly credited in the list of illustrations), the publishers have been enabled to represent many of the most popular paintings by the artist, and a selection of his famous designs for Dalziel's Bible Gallery.

FREDERIC LORD LEIGHTON, P.R.A.

LIST OF DIGNITIES AND HONOURS CONFERRED
ON FREDERIC LEIGHTON.

Knighted, 1878; created a Baronet, 1886; created Baron Leighton of
Stretton, 1896; elected Associate of the Royal Academy, 1864;
Royal Academician, 1869; President of the Royal Academy, 1878;
Hon. Mem. Royal Scottish Academy, and Royal Hibernian
Academy, Associate of the Institute of France, President of the
International Jury of Painting, Paris Exhibition, 1878; Hon.
Member, Berlin Academy, 1886; also Member of the Royal
Academy of Vienna, 1888, Belgium, 1886, of the Academy of St.
Luke, Rome, and the Aca- demies of Florence (1882), Turin,
Genoa, Perugia, and Antwerp (1885); Hon. D.C.L., Oxford, 1879;
Hon. LL.D., Cambridge, 1879; Hon. LL.D., Edinburgh, 1884;
Hon. D.Lit., Dublin, 1892; Hon. D.C.L., Durham, 1894; Hon.
Fellow of Trinity College, London, 1876; Lieut.-Colonel of the 20th
Middlesex (Artists') Rifle Volunteers, 1876 to 1883 (resigned); then
Hon. Colonel and holder of the Volunteer Decoration;
Commander of the Legion of Honour, 1889; Commander of the
Order of Leopold; Knight of the Prussian Order "pour le Mérite,"
and of the Coburg Order Dem Verdienste.

FREDERIC LORD LEIGHTON, P.R.A.

AN ILLUSTRATED CHRONICLE

CHAPTER I

His Early Years

To Italy, at whose liberal well-head English Art has so often renewed itself, we turn naturally for an opening to this chronicle of a great English artist's career. Frederic Leighton was the painter of our time who strove hardest to keep alive an Italian ideal of beauty in London; therefore it is in Italy, the Italy of Raphael and Angelo and his favourite Giotteschi, that we must seek the true beginnings of his art.

London made its first acquaintance with him and his painting in 1855, when the picture, *Cimabue's Madonna carried in Procession through the Streets of Florence*, startled the Royal Academy, and proved that a 'prentice work could be in its way something of a masterpiece. This picture, the work of an unknown young artist of twenty-five, painted chiefly in Rome, showed at once a new force and a new quality, and in its singular feeling for certain of the archaic Italian schools, showed, too, where for the moment the sympathies of the painter really lay. How far the potentiality disclosed in it was developed during the forty years following, how far the ideals in art, which it seemed to declare, were pursued or departed from, the Royal Academy year by year is witness. Here, before we turn to consider the history of those later years, we shall find it interesting to use this first picture as an index to that period of probation, which is so often the most interesting part of an artist's history. In accounting for it, and finding out the determining experiences of the artist's pupilage, we shall account, also, for much that came after. Although Frankfort and Paris play their part, the formative influences of that early period, we shall find, carry us chiefly, and again and again, into Italy.

Frederic Leighton was born on the 3rd of December, 1830, at Scarborough, the son of a medical practitioner. His father, Dr. Frederic Leighton, was also the son of a physician who was knighted for eminence in his profession. Thus we have two generations of medicine and culture in the family; but there is no sign of art, or love for art, before the third. This generation produced three children, all devoted to the graphic arts and to music, of whom the boy, Frederic was the eldest.

A word or two more must be given to his forbears, on grounds of character and heredity, before we pass. Sir James Leighton, the grandfather, was Physician to the Court at St. Petersburg, where he served in succession Alexander the First, and Nicholas, with whom he was on terms of considerable intimacy. His son, Dr. Frederic Leighton, who promised to be a still more brilliant practioner, was educated at Stonyhurst, but after taking his M.D. degree at Edinburgh, just as he was rapidly acquiring the highest professional reputation, contracted a cold that led to a partial deafness. This made it impossible for him to go on practising with safety, and retiring to his study he turned from physical to metaphysical pursuits. In spite of his deafness, as severe an embargo on social reputation as can well be laid, Dr. Leighton is said to have been equally noted among his friends for his keen intellectual quality and his urbanity.

To be the son of his father, then, counted for something in our hero's career. Even in art, which Dr. Leighton did not care for particularly, the boy had very great opportunities. Before he was ten years old, he went abroad with his mother, who was in ill health; and already he had shown such decided signs of the *furor pingendi* during a chance visit to Mr. Lance's studio in Paris, that it is without surprise that we hear of him in 1840 as taking drawing lessons from Signor F. Meli, at Rome. During these early travels the boy's sketch books were full (we are told) of precociously clever things. The climacteric moment came early in his career. At Florence, in 1844, when he was fourteen, he delivered himself of a sort of boyish ultimatum to his father, who, after taking counsel of Hiram Powers, the American sculptor, wisely gave the boy his wish, and decided to let him be an artist. Powers when asked, "Shall I make him an artist?" exclaimed in no uncertain terms, "Sir, you have no choice in the matter, he is one already;" and on further question, the father being anxious about the boy's possibilities, said, "He may become as eminent as he pleases."

Few art students of our time appear to have encountered more fortunate conditions, on the whole, than did Frederic Leighton in the years immediately following. The Florentine school of fifty years ago, however, was not the best for a beginner. It was full of mannerisms, which a boy of that age was sure to pick up, and exaggerate on his own account. At that time Bezzuoli and Servolini were the great lights and directors of the Academy of the Fine Arts, and they delighted, naturally, in so able and so apt a pupil; that he found it hard to shake off their teaching becomes evident later.

Those who had the good fortune at any time to have heard Lord Leighton describe his early wanderings in Europe, must have been struck by the warmth of his tribute to Johann Eduard Steinle, the Frankfort master, who did more than any other to correct his style, and to decide the whole future bent of his art.

Steinle, whose name is barely known to us in England, was one of that remarkable school of painters, called familiarly "the Nazarenes," because of their religious range of subjects, who were inspired originally by Overbeck and Pfühler. Leighton in recent years described him as "an intensely fervent Catholic;" a man of most striking personality, and of most courtly manners, whose influence upon younger men was fairly magnetic. In the case of this particular pupil, certainly, his intervention was of most powerful effect. Religious in his methods, as well as in his sentiment of art, the florid insincerities and mannerisms of the Florentine Academy, as they were still to be seen in the young Leighton's work, found in him an admirable chastener, but it took many years of painfully hard work, lasting until 1852, to undo the evil wrought by decadent Florence.

Prior to this fortunate intercourse with Steinle, the student had an old acquaintance with Frankfort, which, like Florence, seemed destined to play a great part in his history. Before going to Florence, and deciding on his artistic career, in 1844, he had been sent to school in Frankfort. He returned there from Florence to resume his general education, and on leaving at seventeen, went for a year to the Städtelsches Institut.

In 1848 he went to Brussels, and worked there for a time without any master, painting the first picture that deserves to be remembered. Characteristically enough, this depicted *Cimabue finding Giotto in the fields of Florence*. The shepherd boy is engaged in drawing the figure of a lamb upon a smooth rock, using a piece of coal for pencil; an admirable and precocious piece of work. At the time it was first shown it was considered especially good in its harmonious and original colouring, nor did a sight of it in 1896 at the Winter Exhibition of the Royal Academy contradict the generous verdict of contemporary critics. At Brussels he painted a portrait of himself, a notable thing of its kind, wherein we see a slight, dark youth, with a face of much charm and distinction, whose features one easily sees to be like those of later portraits. Then, immediately before the return to Frankfort, and the studying there, under Steinle, Leighton spent some months in Paris, working in an atelier in the Rue Richer.

The conditions of this most informal of life-schools were such as Henri Murger, who was alive and writing at the time, might have approved, but were hardly to be called educative in any higher sense. The only master that these Bohemians could boast was a very invertebrate old artist, who seems to have been the soul of politeness and irresponsibility, and who accompanied every weak criticism with the deprecatory conclusion, "Voilà mon opinion!"

"M. Voilà mon opinion!" is a type not unknown otherwhere than in that Paris atelier. A fine alterative the student must have found the severe and stringent tonics that Steinle prescribed immediately afterwards in Frankfort.

In the admirable monograph on "Sir Frederic Leighton" by Mrs. Andrew Lang, from which we have drawn on occasion in these pages, an interesting account is given of an exploit at Darmstadt, in which the young artist took a chief part. An artists' festival was to be held there, and Sir Frederic and one of his fellow-students, Signor Gamba, took it into their heads to paint a picture for the occasion on the walls of an old ruined castle near the town. The design was speedily sketched after the most approved mediæval fashion, and no time was lost in executing the work. "The subject was a knight standing on the threshold of the castle, welcoming the guests, while in the centre of the picture was Spring, receiving the representatives of the three arts, all of them caricatures of well-known figures. In one corner were the two young artists themselves, surveying the pageant. The Schloss where this piece was painted is still in existence, and the Grand Duke has lately erected a wooden roof over the painting, to preserve it from destruction."

Before leaving Frankfort, Leighton had already interested Steinle in his projected picture of *Cimabue's Madonna*, and the design for it was made under Steinle's direction. Under his direct influence, too, and inspired by Boccaccio, another Florentine picture – a cartoon of its great plague – was painted. In speaking of the dramatic treatment of its subject, Mrs. Lang describes "the contrast between the merry revellers on one side of the picture and the death-cart and its pile of corpses on the other, while in the centre is the link between the two – a terror-stricken woman attempting to escape with her baby from the pestilence-stricken city. We shall look in vain among the President's later works for any picture with a similar *motif*. In general he shared Plato's opinion – that violent passions are unsuitable subjects for art; not so much because the sight of them is degrading, as because what is at once hideous and transitory in its nature should not be perpetuated."

We have seen how the spirit and sentiment of Italy continually remained by the artist in his German studio, and how in Frankfort his artistic imagination returned again and again to Florence, and to the early Florentines of his particular adoration – Cimabue and Giotto. The recall to Italy came inevitably, as Steinle's teaching at last had fully worked its purpose. Steinle himself counselled the move, and gave his favourite pupil an introduction to Cornelius in Rome. It was to Rome, therefore, and not to Florence, that the young artist went – to Rome where sooner or later the steps of all men who work for art or for religion tend, and where so few stay. This was in 1852, the year which was represented in the Commemorative Exhibition at Burlington House by *A Persian Pedlar*, a small full-length figure of a man in Oriental costume, seated cross-legged on a divan, with a long pipe in his hand. To 1853 belongs a *Portrait of Miss Laing* (Lady Nias), which was shown again at the same time.

The Rome of the mid-century was Rome at its best, with much artistic stimulus of the present, as well as of the past. The English colony was particularly strong. Thackeray was there, moving about after his wont in the studios and salons; the Brownings were there, and in their prime. The young painter and his work, including the *Cimabue's Madonna* in its earlier stages, made a great impression on Thackeray, who turned prophet for once on the strength of it. On returning to London and meeting Millais, he prophesied gaily to that ardent Pre-Raphaelite, then marching on from success to success: "Millais! my boy, I have met in Rome a versatile young dog called Leighton, who will one of these days run you hard for the presidentship!" This was early days for such a rumour to reach the Academy, who knew an older1 school, represented by Landseer and Eastlake, and a younger school, represented by Millais and Rossetti, but as yet knew not Leighton.

Among the leading artists in Rome at this time, beside Cornelius, were the two French painters, Bouguereau and Gerome. To these, especially to Bouguereau, who was a great believer in "scientific composition," Leighton was, on his own testimony, largely indebted for his fine sense of form. Yet another famous Frenchman, Robert Fleury, whom he afterwards met in Paris, may be mentioned here, since from him he learnt much in the way of colouring, and the technique of his art.

Turning from the painters to the poets, it was at Rome that Robert Browning, who was at this time writing his "Men and Women," formed close acquaintance with the young artist. Something of the atmosphere which permeates such poems as "Bishop Blougram's Apology," "Andrea del Sarto," and others of the same series, seems to linger yet in the record of those early meetings of poets and painters, with all their associations:

"The Vatican,
Greek busts, Venetian paintings, Roman walls,
And English books."

One easily supposes Browning speaking through his Bishop Blougram, as, it is said, he was heard to speak in those days in praise of Correggio, to whose qualities, Ruskin tells us, Sir Frederic Leighton curiously approximates:

"'Twere pleasant could Correggio's fleeting glow
Hang full in face of one where'er one roams,
Since he more than the others brings with him
Italy's self – the marvellous Modenese!"

Italy's self, in truth, Frederic Leighton, like Browning in poetry, did not fail to bring with him, and revived for us for many years, by his art and southern glow of colour, in the gray heart of London.

Among other people whom Leighton met in Rome were George Sand, Mrs. Kemble, George Mason the painter, of *Harvest Moon* fame, Gibson the sculptor, and Lord Lyons. Like Robert Browning, let us add, he was readily responsive to the quickening of his contemporaries, and vigorously studied the present in order that he might the better paint the past, and put live souls into the archaic raiment of Cimabue and old Florence.

He was working hard all this while, with a devotion and concentration that impressed other friends beside Thackeray, upon his picture of *Cimabue's Madonna*, which was exhibited in the Academy of 1855, and as the work of an unknown hand made a distinct sensation. It was discussed, angrily by some, delightedly by others. The criticism which Rossetti, Mr. Ruskin, and other critics bestowed upon it in the press or in private correspondence[1] will come more fitly into our later pages, when we turn to deal with contemporary opinions upon Leighton's work. Enough to say here that it won fame for the artist at a stroke. The Queen bought it for £600, having bespoken it, I believe, before it left his studio, and hung it eventually in Buckingham Palace. With this encouraging first great success, the probationary stage of our artist's history may be said to close.

CHAPTER II

Year by Year – 1855 to 1864

The Academy of forty years ago was very different from that we know to-day. It was held in the left wing of the National Gallery, and had not nearly so much space at its disposal as it has in its present quarters at Burlington House. The exhibition of 1855 contained few pictures, compared with the multitudinous items of the present shows.

Generally speaking, the exhibition was of a heavier, more Georgian aspect, in spite of certain Pre-Raphaelite experiments and other signs of the coming of a younger generation. Sir Charles Eastlake was President. Professor Hart was delivering lectures to its students, full of academic, respectable intelligence, if little more; lectures which those who are curious may find reported in full in the "Athenæum" of that time.

More interesting was the appearance of Mr. Ruskin as commentator on the pictures of the Academy in this year, the first in which he issued his characteristic "Academy Notes." His long, and, all things considered, remarkably appreciative criticism of the *Cimabue's Madonna* we discuss elsewhere. Of another picture of Italy by a very different painter, which was considered a masterpiece by some critics, we find him speaking in terms of monition: "Is it altogether too late to warn him that he is fast becoming nothing more than an Academician?" The one picture of the year, according to Mr. Ruskin, was the *Rescue*, by Millais. "It is the only great picture exhibited this year," he writes, "but this is very great." For the rest, *A Scene from As You Like It*, by Maclise; another Shakespearean subject, the inevitable *Lear and Cordelia*, by Herbert; and a *Beatrice* by the then President, and we have recalled everything that served to give the Academy of that year its distinction in the eyes of contemporary critics. Sir Edwin Landseer, who to the outer world was the one great fact in the art of the time, does not appear to have exhibited in 1855.

Looking back now to that date, what one discerns chiefly is the emergence of the Pre-Raphaelites from the more conventional multitude that were taking up the artistic traditions of the first half of the century. Millais, Rossetti, Holman Hunt, and their associates, count to us, to-day, as the representatives of an earlier generation; in 1855 they still stood for all that was daring, unprecedented, and adventurous in their art.

This newcomer, with his *Cimabue's Madonna* in a new style, puzzled the critics considerably. They did not know quite how to allot him in their casual division of contemporary schools. "Landseer and Maclise we know; and Millais and Holman Hunt; but who is Leighton?" was the tenor of their commentary.

Meanwhile an event of great significance to English Art in this year was happening – an exhibition of English pictures in Paris, the first of its kind. This beginning of such international exchanges was important; it has led up to many striking modifications of both English and French schools since that date. It is curious that it should coincide with the awakening to certain other foreign influences: that of the early Italian school upon the Pre-Raphaelites, and that of the later Italian, popularly known as "the classic school," upon Leighton and Mr. G. F. Watts.

Of this exhibition of English pictures, which was held in the Avenue Montaigne, M. Ernest Chesneau, a critic very sympathetic to English art, tells us, in his admirable book on the

"English School of Painting," that "for the French it was a revelation of a style and a school of the very existence of which they had hitherto had no idea; and whether owing to its novelty, or the surprise it occasioned, or, indeed, to its real merit, whatever may have been the true cause, most certain it is that the English, until then little thought of and almost unknown abroad, obtained in France a great success."

M. Chesneau, in going on to account further for the great impression made by the English painters in Paris, attributes it largely to the *singularity* which, for foreign eyes, marks their work. It is curious, indeed, that French critics, and M. Chesneau among them, really admire this singularity, which they count distinctively British. They look for it in our pictures, and if they do not find it – as in the work of Leighton – they feel aggrieved.

British eccentricity, whether thinking its way with the aid of genius into "Pre-Raphaelitism," or now again, with the aid of extreme cleverness and talent, into certain cruder forms of "impressionism," is sure of its effect. But an art like Leighton's, whose aim is beauty and not eccentricity, is apt to be slighted by both French and English critics, with some notable exceptions. Not all its grace, its classic quality, its beauty of line and distinction of treatment, avail it, when it comes into conflict with doctrinaire theories on the one hand, and a love for mere sensationalism on the other.

The success of his picture at the Academy, and the incidental lionizing of a season, did not tempt the artist to stay long in London, and he went to Paris, where he settled himself in a studio and proceeded to complete his *Triumph of Music,* and other pictures begun in Rome.

By this time the painter's method might seem assured, but Paris was still able to add something to his style, with the aid of such masters as Fleury. English critics, who expected *The Triumph of Music* to sustain the reputation won by *Cimabue's Madonna,* were disappointed – partly because Orpheus was represented as playing a violin, in place of the traditional lyre. To those who will examine and compare them more carefully, there is no such discrepancy. *The Triumph of Music: Orpheus by the power of his Art redeems his wife from Hades,* which is every whit as distinctive a performance as the *Cimabue's Madonna* (as indeed it was conceived and painted largely under the same conditions), was nevertheless not a popular success. Certainly, it marks, as clearly as anything can, the sense of colour, the sense of form, the draughtsmanship, the immensely cultured eye and hand, first discovered to the English critics by its predecessor. It was sold after the painter's death.

Of certain other works painted in 1856, 1857, and 1858, some of which never found their way to the Academy, little need be said. To this period belong two pictures painted in Paris, the one, *Pan* under a fig-tree, with a quotation from Keats's "Endymion":

"O thou, to whom
Broad-leaved fig-trees even now foredoom
Their ripened heritage,"

and the other, a pendant to it, *A Nymph and Cupid*.

Salome, the Daughter of Herodias, painted in 1857, but apparently not exhibited at the Academy, represents a small full-length figure in white drapery, with her arms above her head, which is crowned with flowers; behind her stands a female musician. Another, shown in 1858 at the Royal Academy, and again in the 1897 retrospective exhibition, was first entitled *The Fisherman and Syren,* and afterwards *The Mermaid*; it is a composition of two small full-length figures, a mermaid clasping a fisherman round the neck. The subject is taken from a ballad by Goethe:

"Half drew she him,
Half sunk he in,
And never more was seen."

In the same year was a painting inspired by "Romeo and Juliet," entitled *Count Paris, accompanied by Friar Laurence, comes to the house of the Capulets to claim his bride; he finds Juliet stretched, apparently lifeless, on the bed.* The picture shows, in addition to the figures named in its former title, the father and mother of Juliet bending over their daughter's body, and through an opening beyond numerous figures at the foot of the staircase.

The latter year marked the painter's return to London, where he entered more actively into its artistic life than he had done hitherto, and made closer acquaintance with the Pre-Raphaelites, who were already entering upon their second and maturer stage. To take Rossetti: it was in 1856 that he made those five notable designs to illustrate "Poems by Alfred Tennyson," which Moxon and Co. published in the following year; an event that, for the first time, really introduced him to the public at large. To 1857, again, belongs Rossetti's *Blue Closet* and *Damsel of the Sangrael,* both painted for Mr. W. Morris. And in 1857 and 1858, the famous and hapless distemper pictures on the walls of the Union Debating Society's room at Oxford, were engaging Rossetti and his associates, including Burne-Jones, William Morris, Mr. Val. Prinsep, Mr. Arthur Hughes, and Mr. Spencer Stanhope.

It was in the summer of 1858, Mr. F. G. Stephens tells us, that the original Hogarth Club was founded, of which the two Rossettis were prominent instigators, – one of the most notable of the many protestant societies that have sprung up at different times from a slightly anti-Academic bias. It is interesting to find that Leighton's famous *Lemon Tree* drawing in silverpoint was exhibited here. The Hogarth Club held its meetings at 178, Piccadilly, in the first instance; removed afterwards to 6, Waterloo Place, Pall Mall, and finally dissolved, in 1861, after existing for four seasons.

To speak of other painters more or less associated with Rossetti and his school, Mr. Holman Hunt, whose *Light of the World* had greatly struck Paris in 1855, exhibited his *Scapegoat* at the Academy of 1856, a picture which called from Mr. Ruskin immense praise, and a characteristic protest: "I pray him to paint a few pictures with less feeling in them, and more handling." Of Millais we have already spoken. In 1856 he exhibited *The Child of the Regiment, Peace Concluded*, and *Autumn Leaves*.

In 1859 Leighton showed three pictures at the Academy. One, *A Roman Lady* (then called *La Nanna*), a half-length black-haired figure, facing the spectator, in Italian costume; another, now called *Nanna*, then entitled *Pavonia*, a half-length figure of a girl in Italian costume, with peacock's feathers in the background; and *Sunny Hours*, which seems to have escaped record so far. The same year saw another of his pictures, *Samson and Delilah*, exhibited at Suffolk Street.

We must not pass by the famous *Study of a Lemon Tree* (now at Oxford), mentioned above, without quoting the praise by Mr. Ruskin, which made it famous. Mr. Ruskin couples it with another drawing, both of which we have been fortunately able to reproduce in our pages. These "two perfect early drawings," he writes, "are of *A Lemon Tree*, and another of the same date, of *A Byzantine Well*, which determine for you without appeal, the question respecting necessity of delineation as the first skill of a painter. Of all our present masters Sir Frederic Leighton delights most in softly-blended colours, and his ideal of beauty is more nearly that of Correggio than any seen since Correggio's time. But you see by what precision of terminal outline he at first restrained, and exalted, his gift of beautiful *vaghezza*." The *Lemon Tree* study, let us add, was drawn at Capri in the spring of 1859. Here, and elsewhere in the South of Europe, whither the artist returned, escaping from London at every opportunity, many other notable studies and drawings were made during this period. Some of these were employed long since for the backgrounds of pictures familiar to us all. Others, faithful studies of nature, small oil and water-colour drawings, chiefly landscape, were scarce known to the general public during the painter's life, but were eagerly competed for at the sale of his pictures in July, 1896.

The little picture of *Capri at Sunrise* was hung in the Academy of 1860, the painter's only contribution of that year. In the year following, we find another small picture of Capri, together with five others, some of which played their part in winning for the artist his wider recognition.

Meanwhile, the artist was drawing his London ties closer. In 1860 he took up his abode at 2, Orme Square, where he continued to reside until he built his famous house in Holland Park Road, some years later. His art did not for this reason become more like London, or more infected with that British singularity which some critics would seem to demand. On the contrary, Italy and the South, the glow of colour, the perfection of form, the plastic exquisiteness, which mark for us his mature performances, and which follow after classic ideals, were more and more clearly to be discerned in the remarkable cycle of pictures associated with this part of his career.

In 1861 he painted portraits of his sister, *Mrs. Sutherland Orr*, and of *Mr. John Hanson Walker*, the former shown at the Academy, where also hung *Paolo e Francesca, A Dream, Lieder ohne Worte, J. A. - a Study*, and *Capri - Paganos*. Rossetti, writing of this exhibition, says: "Leighton might, as you say, have made a burst had not his pictures been ill-placed mostly – indeed, one of them (the only very good one, *Lieder ohne Worte*) is the only instance of very striking unfairness in the place."[2] In 1862 there were no fewer than six of the artist's pictures at the May exhibition of the Academy: the *Odalisque*, a very popular work, shows a draped female figure, in a very Leightonesque pose, with her arm above her head, leaning against a wall by the water. She holds a peacock's feather screen in her left hand, while a swan in the water at her feet cranes its head upwards towards her; *Michael Angelo nursing his dying Servant*, a group of two three-quarter length figures; the servant reclining in an armchair with his head resting against the shoulder of Michael Angelo – a fairly powerful but somewhat academic version of the incident – which looks at first glance like the work of a not very important "old master;" *The Star of Bethlehem*, showing one of the Magi on the terrace of his house looking at the strange star in the East, while below are indications of a revel he has just left. *Duett, Sisters, Sea Echoes*, and

Rustic Music, also belong to this year.

In 1863 he showed *Eucharis,* a half-length figure of a white-robed girl, with a basket of fruit on her head; *Jezebel and Ahab; A Cross-bow Man;* and *A Girl Feeding Peacocks;* with these we complete the list of his work as an outsider.

CHAPTER III

Year by Year – 1864 to 1869

In 1864 Leighton was made an Associate of the Royal Academy. To its summer exhibition he contributed three pictures, showing great and various power in their composition. *Dante at Verona*, *Orpheus and Eurydice*, and *Golden Hours*. The first of these, one of the most remarkable pictures of our modern English school, in which "Dante" appears, is a large work, with figures something less than life-size. It illustrates the verses in the "Paradiso":

> "Thou shalt prove
> How salt the savour is of others' bread;
> How hard the passage, to descend and climb
> By others' stairs. But that shall gall thee most
> Will be the worthless and vile company
> With whom thou must be thrown into the straits,
> For all ungrateful, impious all and mad
> Shall turn against thee."

"Dante, in fulfilment of this prophecy, is seen descending the palace stairs of the Can Grande, at Verona, during his exile. He is dressed in sober grey and drab clothes, and contrasts strongly in his ascetic and suffering aspect with the gay revellers about him. The people are preparing for a festival, and splendidly and fantastically robed, some bringing wreaths of flowers. Bowing with mock reverence, a jester gibes at Dante. An indolent sentinel is seated at the porch, and looks on unconcernedly, his spear lying across his breast. A young man, probably acquainted with the writing of Dante, sympathises with him. In the centre and just before the feet of Dante, is a beautiful child, brilliantly dressed and crowned with flowers, and dragging along the floor a garland of bay leaves and flowers, while looking earnestly and innocently in the poet's face. Next come a pair of lovers, the lady looking at Dante with attention, the man heedless. The last wears a vest embroidered with eyes like those in a peacock's tail. A priest and a noble descend the stairs behind, jeering at Dante."[3]

It was the *Golden Hours* which, though perhaps less memorable and imaginative than the others, won the greatest popular success of the three, a success beyond anything that the artist had so far painted. As this picture is here reproduced, description is needless, except so far as regards the colour of the background, which is literally golden. The dress of the lady who leans upon the spinet is white, embroidered with flowers. The *Orpheus and Eurydice* showed that the old friendship, formed originally in Rome, between the painter and Robert Browning, was maintained. Some of the poet's lines served as a text for the picture; and as they are little known we repeat them here:

"But give them me – the mouth, the eyes, the brow –
Let them once more absorb me! One look now
Will lap me round for ever, not to pass
Out of its light, though darkness lie beyond.
Hold me but safe again within the bond
Of one immortal look! All woe that was,
Forgotten, and all terror that may be,
Defied, – no past is mine, no future! look at me!"

To this year, also, belongs a portrait of *The late Miss Lavinia I'Anson*, a circular panel showing the sky for background. This was exhibited again in the winter Academy of 1897.

In 1865 the artist showed once again his eclectic sympathies, by the variety of the subject-pictures that he sent to the Academy, ranging from *David* to *Helen of Troy*.

In his tenderly conceived *David*, the Psalmist is seen gazing at two doves in the sky above; he, sunk in a profound reverie, is seated upon a house-top overlooking some neighbouring hills. The whole is large in its handling and treatment, and in the simplicity of its drapery recalls several of the famous illustrations the artist contributed to Dalziel's Bible Gallery. It was exhibited with the quotation, "Oh, that I had wings like a dove! for then would I fly away and be at rest." With the delightful *Helen of Troy* we are recalled to the third book of the Iliad, when Iris bids Helen go and see the general truce made pending the duel between Paris and Menelaus, of which she is to be the prize. So Helen, having summoned her maids and "shadowed her graces with white veils," rose and passed along the ramparts of Troy. In the picture the light falls on her shoulders and her hair, while her face and the whole of the front of her form are shadowed over, with somewhat mystical effect.

To the same year belongs *In St. Mark's*, a picture of a lady with a child in her arms leaving the church, a lovely and finished study of colour; *The Widow's Prayer*; and *Mother and Child*, a graceful reminder of a gentler world than Helen's.

In 1866 the critics had at last a work which seemed to them to follow the lines of the *Cimabue's Madonna*. This was the radiant and lovely picture of the *Syracusan Bride leading Wild Beasts in Procession to the Temple of Diana*. The composition of this remarkable painting deserves to be closely studied, for it is very characteristic of Sir Frederic Leighton's theories of art, and his conviction of the necessarily decorative effect of such works. A terrace of white marble, whose line is reflected and repeated by the line of white clouds in the sky painting above, affords the figures of the procession a delightful setting. The Syracusan bride leads a lioness, and these are followed by a train of maidens and wild beasts, the last reduced to a pictorial seemliness and decorative calm, very fortunate under the circumstances. The procession is seen approaching the door of the temple, and a statue of Diana serves as a last note in the ideal harmonies of form and colour to which the whole is attuned. As compared with the

Cimabue's Madonna, it is a more finished piece of work, and the handling throughout is more assured. It was as much an advance, technically, upon that, as the *Daphnephoria*, which crowned the artist's third decade, was upon this. According to popular report, it was this picture of the *Syracusan Bride* which decided his future election as a full member of the Academy; but as a matter of fact, it was in 1869 that this election took place. The picture, let us add, was suggested to the painter by a passage in the second Idyll of Theocritus: "And for her then many other wild beasts were going in procession round about, and among them a lioness." *The Painter's Honeymoon* and a *Portrait of Mrs. James Guthrie* were also exhibited this year; and the wall-painting of *The Wise and Foolish Virgins*, at Lyndhurst, in the New Forest, was executed during the summer.

In its next exhibition, that of 1867, the Academy held five pictures by the artist, including the delightful *Pastoral*, two small full-length figures standing in a landscape of a shepherd and a girl – whom he is teaching to play the pipes. This again might be considered a painter's translation from Theocritus, and the *Venus Disrobing for the Bath*, one of the most debated of all the artist's paintings of the nude. The paleness of the flesh-tint of this Venus aroused a criticism which has often been urged against his pictures – that such a hue was not in nature. In imparting an ideal effect to an ideal subject, Leighton always, however, followed his own conviction – that art has a law of its own, and a harmony of colour and form, derived and selected no doubt from natural loveliness, but not to be referred too closely to the natural, or to the average, in these things.

To the 1868 Academy Leighton contributed another biblical theme, *Jonathan's Token to David*. With this were four others, as widely varying in subject and conception as need be desired. One was a very charming portrait of a very pretty woman, *Mrs. Frederick P. Cockerell*. Then follow three more in that cycle of classic subjects, of which the painter never tired. The full title of the first runs, *Ariadne abandoned by Theseus: Ariadne watches for his return: Artemis releases her by death.* In it the figure of Ariadne, clothed in white drapery, is seen lying on a rocky promontory overlooking the sea. *Acme and Septimius* is a circular picture, with two small full-length figures reclining on a marble bench. This extract from Sir Theodore Martin's translation of Catullus was appended to its title in the catalogue:

> "Then bending gently back her head,
> With that sweet mouth so rosy red,
> Upon his eyes she dropped a kiss,
> Intoxicating him with bliss."

A love song on canvas, a pictorial transcript from Catullus, it was perhaps the most popular picture of the year. The last of the three was *Actæa, the Nymph of the Shore.* It represents a small full-length nude figure lying on white drapery by the sea-shore. Actæa is a lovely figure, full of that grace which Leighton so well knew how to impart to his idealized figures.

After this year, at any rate, there could be no longer any doubt but that the artist's power really lay in the creation of ideal forms; whether presented in monomime or combined in poetic and decorative groups, called up from the wonderful limbo of classic myth and history.

With 1869 came *Electra at the Tomb of Agamemnon,* a memorable picture, full of characteristic effects of colour and composition, and a notable exercise in the grand style. This work, considered from any side, must be seen to be the outcome of a unique faculty, so unprecedented in English art as to run every risk of misconception that native predilections could impose upon those who stopped to criticise it. The figure of Electra clad in black drapery offered a problem of peculiar difficulty.

Another painting shown this year was *Dædalus and Icarus,* a strikingly conceived picture. The two figures are singularly noble conceptions of the idealized nude; the drapery at the back of Icarus is typical of the painter in every fold, while the landscape seen far below the stone platform on which the figures stand, shows a bay of the blue Ægean sea in full sidelight, with a lovely glimpse of the white walls of a distant town.

The same exhibition of 1869 saw, also, the vigorously painted diploma picture, *St. Jerome*, which marked his election as R.A. In it the saint, nude to the waist, kneels with uplifted arms at the foot of a crucifix, his lion seen in the background. *Helios and Rhodos*, another painting exhibited at the same time, shows Helios descending from his chariot, which is in a cloud above, to embrace the nymph Rhodos, who has risen from the sea.

CHAPTER IV

Year by Year – 1870 to 1878

Sundry journeys into the East during this period of Leighton's career, gave him new subject-matter, new tints to his palette, and added something of an oriental fantasy to the classic sentiment of his art. The sketches of Damascus and other time-honoured eastern cities, mosques, gardens, and courtyards, which figured largely among Sir Frederic's studies, were made for the most part in the autumn of 1873.

Previously, as early as 1867, the East had cast its spell upon him. In 1868, he went into Egypt, and made a voyage up the Nile with M. de Lesseps, then at the flood of good-fortune. The Khedive himself provided the steamer for this adventure. "It was during this voyage," we are told, "that Sir Frederic came across a small child with the strangest and most limited idea of full dress that probably ever occurred to mortal – a tiny coin strung on to one of her strong coarse hairs." Of the studies made during the journey, one is a woman's head, draped so as to have a singularly archaic and Sphinx-like effect, Another is the fine profile of a young peasant; and yet another, the head of an old man, simple-minded and philosophical.

In 1869 the *Helios and Rhodos*, already mentioned, served as the first sign to the public of the new R.A.'s interest in things oriental. To the 1870 exhibition, his only contribution was the picture, *A Nile Woman*, which is now owned by the Princess of Wales. It is a small full-length figure of a girl, balancing an empty pitcher upon her head, at the time of moonrise. Anticipating the Eastern subjects which future years produced, we may note a picture of *Old Damascus*, showing the Jews' quarter in that fabled city, in all its motley picturesqueness, and the delightful *Moorish Garden, – A Dream of Granada*, which were exhibited in 1874. A powerful picture, shown in 1875, of the *Egyptian Slinger*,[4] is illustrated later in this volume, but no reproduction can quite suggest the striking colouring of the original, and the masterly treatment of its light and shade, in the presentment of this lonely figure posed high on its platform against the clear evening sky. The delightful *Little Fatima*, and the *Grand Mosque, Damascus*, enlarged from the sketch previously alluded to, were also exhibited in 1875.

But perhaps the most picturesque memorial of the East due to the artist's wanderings of these years, is an architectural, and not a pictorial one. The fame of the Arab Hall in Lord Leighton's house has reached even further than that of *Little Fatima*, or his painting of the *Grand Mosque at Damascus*. Built originally to provide a setting for some exquisite blue tiles, brought by the owner from Damascus itself, it remains the most perfect representation of an oriental interior to be found in London; but this again belongs to a later period, and we must return to the date whence this chronicle was interrupted. Before doing so, however, it may be noted that in 1870 began the famous Winter Exhibitions of Old Masters and Deceased British Artists, of which Leighton was one of the most active supporters.

In the May exhibition of the Royal Academy, 1871, was hung a notable canvas, *Greek Girls picking up Pebbles by the Sea*, described at the time as "a delightful composition, comprising figures of almost exhaustless grace, and wealth of beauty in design and colour."

Another painting, also shown there, *Cleoboulos instructing his daughter Cleobouline*, is a charming example of its kind. The philosopher, with a scroll on his lap, sits on a cushioned bench with his young daughter by his side, his earnest action in delightful contrast with her girlish grace.

But his great work in 1871 was *Hercules wrestling with Death for the body of Alcestis*. The scene of this profound tragedy is on the sea-shore, where the body of Alcestis, robed in white, lies under the branches of trees in the centre of the picture. On the left is a group of mourners, a seated girl and a woman prostrate in grief. On the right are the two struggling figures; Hercules' superb form and tossing lion-skin contrasting finely, both in action and colouring, with the tall and coldly grey-robed spectre of Death, who presses forward to the bed where Alcestis lies, whence he is thrust back by the mighty Hercules. The exquisite figure of Alcestis with her statuesquely draped robes and their pure and delicate colouring, forms a wonderful contrast to the two strenuous figures on the right, while the figures of the mourners on the left are delightfully posed and full of grace.

In July of this year, it is interesting to remember, appeared Browning's "Balaustion's Adventure," which contained the following tribute to the above picture and its painter:

"I know, too, a great Kaunian painter, strong
As Herakles, though rosy with a robe
Of grace that softens down the sinewy strength:
And he has made a picture of it all.
There lies Alkestis dead, beneath the sun,
She longed to look her last upon, beside
The sea, which somehow tempts the life in us
To come trip over its white waste of waves,
And try escape from earth, and fleet as free.
Behind the body I suppose there bends
Old Pheres in his hoary impotence;
And women-wailers, in a corner crouch
– Four, beautiful as you four, – yes, indeed!
Close, each to other, agonizing all,
As fastened, in fear's rhythmic sympathy,

To two contending opposite. There strains
The might o' the hero 'gainst his more than match,
– Death, dreadful not in thew and bone, but like
The envenomed substance that exudes some dew,
Whereby the merely honest flesh and blood
Will fester up and run to ruin straight,
Ere they can close with, clasp and overcome,
The poisonous impalpability
That simulates a form beneath the flow
Of those grey garments; I pronounce that piece
Worthy to set up in our Poikilé!"

To 1872 belongs the *Summer Moon*, one of the loveliest things ever shown at the Academy, a picture full of that rarer feeling for light and colour, which the artist achieved again and again in his treatment of sunset, twilight, and night effects. *After Vespers*, exhibited the same year, is a three-quarter length figure of a girl in a green robe standing in front of a bench, holding in her right hand a string of beads. This year's Academy held also *A Condottiere*, the noble figure of a man in armour, now in the Birmingham Municipal Gallery, and a portrait of the *Right Hon. Edward Ryan*. Hardly less memorable was *Moretta*, exhibited in the Academy of 1873, in the words of a critic of the day, "one of the most subtle and fortunate productions of the painter." *Moretta* is robed in green, with masses of loosely arranged hair, and a tender and delicate face. *Weaving the Wreath*, shown the same year (and again in the Guildhall, 1895), is a very charming figure of quite a young girl seated on a carpet upon a raised step at the foot of a building. Behind her is a bas-relief, against which her head, crowned by a chaplet of flowers, tells out with sculpturesque effect; the sharp, vertical line of thread strained between her hands, and thence in diagonal line to the ball at her feet, is curiously rigid, and by contrast makes the draperies across which it is silhouetted appear still more mobile.

We are passing over, deliberately, the artist's decorative masterpieces of this period, – the South Kensington frescoes to wit; of which the *Arts of War* belongs to the year 1872, and its companion, *Arts of Peace*, to 1873. These works will be found treated at length in a later chapter on the artist's decorative work (pp. 63, 64).

In the Academy of 1874 appeared four pictures, the most important being the heroic painting, – *Clytemnestra from the Battlements of Argos watches for the Beacon-fires which are to announce the Return of Agamemnon.* In this picture, the figure of Clytemnestra is seen standing erect, with hands folded, supporting the drapery that clothes a majestic form. For further description, we may be content to quote that given at the time in the appreciative art columns of the "Athenæum:"

"There is the grandeur of Greek tragedy in Mr. Leighton's *Clytemnestra* watching for the signal of her husband's return from Troy. The time is deep in the fateful night, while the city sleeps; moonlight floods the walls, the roofs, the gates, and the towers with a ghastly glare, which seems presageful, and casts shadows as dark as they are mysterious and terrible. The dense blue of the sky is dim, sad, and ominous. But the most ominous and impressive element of the picture is a grim figure, the tall woman on the palace roof before us, who looks Titanic in her stateliness, and huge beyond humanity in the voluminous white drapery that wraps her limbs and bosom. Her hands are clenched and her arms thrust down straight and rigidly, each finger locked as in a struggle to strangle its fellow; the muscles swell on the bulky limbs. Drawn erect and with set features, which are so pale that the moonlight could not make them paler, the queen stares fixedly and yet eagerly into the distance, as if she had the will to look over the very edge of the world for the light to come."

Another picture this year was the *Moorish Garden – a dream of Granada*, a delightful little canvas, almost square. In the foreground is a young girl carrying copper vessels, and followed by two peacocks; the background is obviously taken from the study of a garden at Generalife (reproduced at p. 28); the *Antique Juggling Girl* and *Old Damascus: the Jews' Quarter*, were also in the Academy of 1874.

To 1875 belongs the *Egyptian Slinger*, a picture which, as we shall see later, provoked severe censure from Mr. Ruskin. As exhibited it differed much from its present state. Not only was the sky of deeper violet, but almost in silhouette against the moon, on another raised platform, stood a draped female figure, afterwards painted out entirely. Other works shown this year were *Little Fatima*, a small half-length figure of a little girl in Eastern costume, seen against a dark background; and a *Portion of the Interior of the Grand Mosque at Damascus* (reproduced at p. 28). As the building it depicts has since been burnt down, the fine transcript has an added interest. We are come now to a year which, even beyond other years of activity, displayed the artist's characteristic energy: 1876. In the Academy of that year, with the *Daphnephoria*, Leighton once more chose a great classic theme, for a painting which, by its composition, reminded the critics and lovers of art of the artist's early triumph with the *Cimabue's Madonna*, and of his other great processional picture, the *Syracusan Bride*.

Of all his works in this class, there is no doubt that the *Daphnephoria* is the most technically complete. The procession is seen defiling along a terrace backed by trees through which the clear southern sky gleams. A youth carrying the symbolic olive bough, called the Kopo, adorned with its curious emblems, leads the procession. He is clad in purple robes and crowned with leaves. The youthful priest, known as the Daphnephoros (the laurel-bearer) follows, clothed in white raiment. He is similarly crowned, and carries a slim laurel stem. Then come three boys, in scanty red and green draperies, which serve only to emphasize the beauty of their almost naked forms, the middle and tallest one bearing aloft a draped trophy of golden armour. These are seen to be pausing while the leader of the chorus, a tall, finely modelled man, whose back is turned, is giving directions to the chorus with uplifted right hand; in his left hand is a lyre, and the left arm from the elbow is characteristically draped. The first row of the chorus is composed of five children, clothed in purple, crowned with flowers; two rows of maidens, in blue and white, come next; and these in turn are succeeded by some boys with cymbals. The interest of the passing procession is very much enhanced by the effect produced on two lovely bystanders, – a girl and child in blue, beautifully designed, who are drawing water in the left foreground. In the valley below is seen the town of Thebes.

With the painter's reading of the *Daphnephoria* it may be interesting to compare another account of this splendid religious function. At this festival in honour of Apollo, celebrated every ninth year by the Bœotians, it was usual, says pleasant Lempriere,

> "to adorn an olive bough with garlands of laurel and other flowers, and place on the top a brazen globe, from which were suspended smaller ones. In the middle was placed a number of crowns, and a globe of inferior size, and the bottom was adorned with a saffron-coloured garment. The globe on the top represented the Sun, or Apollo; that in the middle was an emblem of the moon, and the others of the stars. The crowns, which were 365 in number, represented the sun's annual revolution. This bough was carried in solemn procession by a beautiful youth of an illustrious family, whose parents were both living. He was dressed in rich garments which reached to the ground, his hair hung loose and dishevelled, his head was covered with a golden crown, and he wore on his feet shoes called *Iphricatidæ*, from Iphricates, an Athenian who first invented them. He was called 'laurel-bearer,' and at that time he executed the office of priest of Apollo. He was preceded by one of his nearest relations, bearing a rod adorned with garlands, and behind him followed a train of virgins with branches in their hands. In this order the procession advanced as far as the temple of Apollo, surnamed Ismenius, where supplicatory hymns were sung to the god."[5]

In the 1876 Academy hung also the striking portrait, *Captain Richard Burton, H.M.'s Consul at Trieste*; and two very characteristic single figures, *Teresina* and *Paolo*. The portrait of Captain Burton has been fairly described as masterly. "There is no attempt," said one critic, "at posing or picturesqueness in the portrait. It is the head of a man who is lean and rugged and brown, but the face is full of character, and every line tells. It is painted in the same strong and bold, and yet careful, way that distinguishes the head of Signor Costa, painted three years later."

The next year saw Leighton's first appearance as a sculptor. It was at the Academy of 1877 that he exhibited the well-known, vigorously designed and wrought *Athlete Struggling with a Python*.[6] This adventure of the R.A. into a new field proved so successful, that the *Athlete* took rank as the most striking piece of sculpture of that year. "In this work," said a friendly critic, "Mr. Leighton has attempted to succeed in a truly antique way. We are bound to admit that he has done wisely, bravely, and successfully." The statue was bought, we may add, for £2,000, as the first purchase made by the trustees of the Chantrey Fund, and is now in the Tate Gallery at Millbank. It was afterwards repeated in marble, by the artist's own hand, for the Danish Museum at Copenhagen.

Still more popular was his *Music Lesson*, another work in the same exhibition. To realize the full charm of this picture, one must see the original; for much depends upon the beauty of its colouring. Imagine a classical marble hall, marble floor, marble walls, in black and white, and red – deep red – marble pillars; and sitting there, sumptuously attired, but bare-footed, two fair-haired girls, who serve for pupil and music-mistress. The elder is showing the younger how to finger a lyre, of exquisite design and finish; and the expression on their faces is charmingly true, while the colours that they contribute to the composition, – the pale blue of the child's dress, the pale flesh tints, the pale yellow hair, and the white and gold of the elder girl's loose robe, and the rich auburn of her hair, – are most harmonious. A bit of scarlet pomegranate blossom, lying on the marble ground, gives the last high note of colour to the picture. Two other pictures of 1877 must not be omitted. *Study* shows us a little girl (the present Lady Orkney), in Eastern garb, diligently reading a sheet of music which lies before her on a little desk. There is great charm in the simple grace of the picture and in the softly brilliant colouring of the child's costume. Very delightful, too, is the portrait of *Miss*

Mabel Mills (now the Hon. Mrs. Grenfell), habited in black velvet, and a large dark hat with coloured feathers, set against a grey background, a picture here reproduced. *A Study, An Italian Girl,* and a *Portrait of H. E. Gordon,* were all three shown at the Grosvenor Gallery the same year.

Another picture, in which a simple theme is treated in a classic fashion – not dissimilar to that employed for the *Music Lesson* – is *Winding the Skein,* a lovely painting exhibited at the Academy in 1878. In this we see two Greek maidens as naturally employed as we often see English girls in other surroundings. This idealization of a familiar occupation – so that it is lifted out of a local and casual sphere, into the permanent sphere of classic art, is characteristic of the whole of Leighton's work. He, like Sir L. Alma-Tadema and Albert Moore, contrived also to preserve a certain modern contemporary feeling in the classic presentment of his themes. He was never archaic; so that the classic scenarium of his subjects, in his hands, appears as little antiquarian as a mediæval environment, shall we say, in the hands of Browning. *Nausicaa,* a full-length girlish figure, in green and white draperies, standing in a doorway, and *Serafina,* another single figure, and *A Study,* were also shown the same year. At the Grosvenor Gallery were a *Portrait of Miss Ruth Stewart Hodgson,* a demure little damsel in outdoor attire, and a *Study of a Girl's Head,* full face.

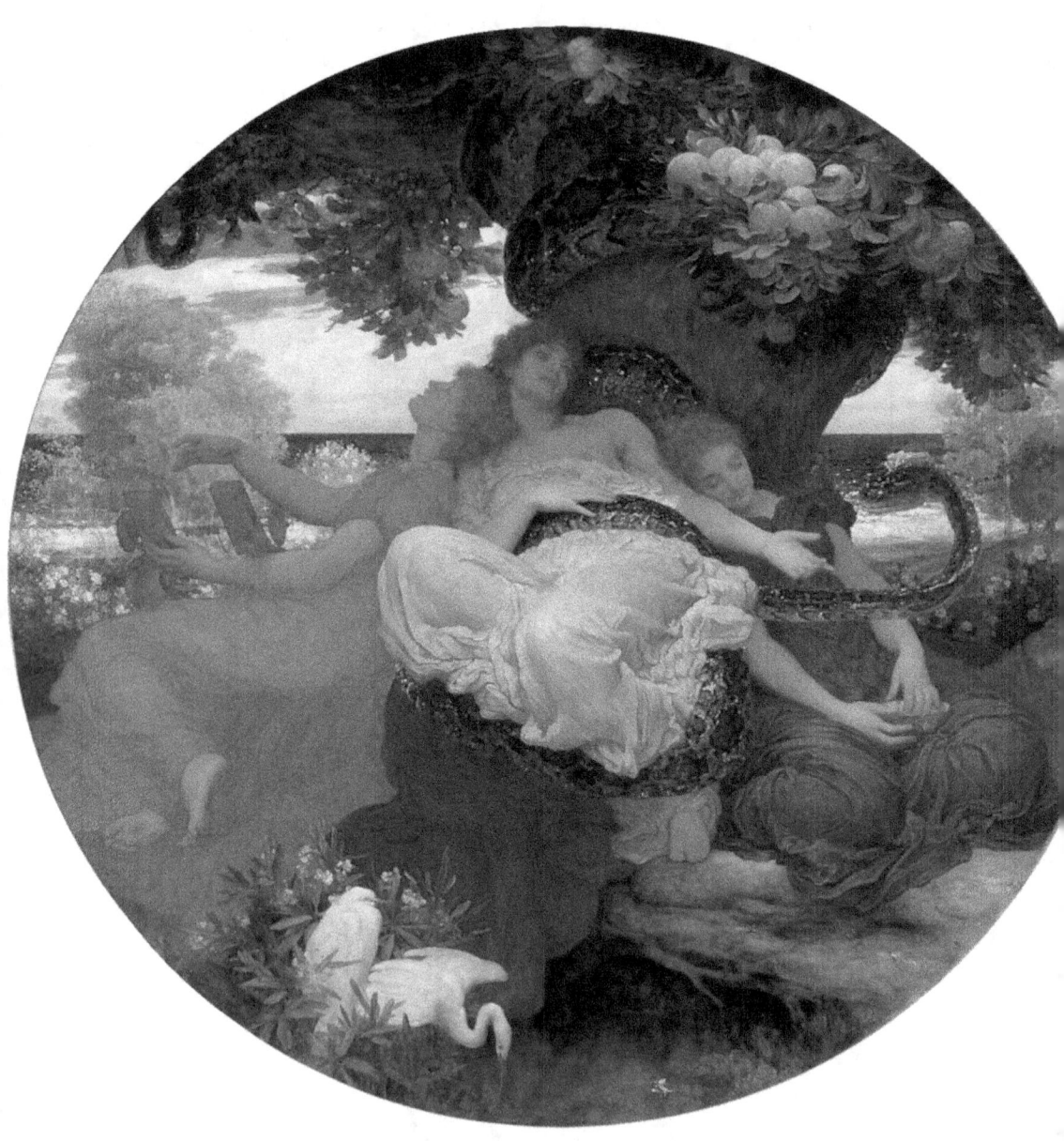

Lord Leighton, The Garden of the
Hesperides, Liverpool

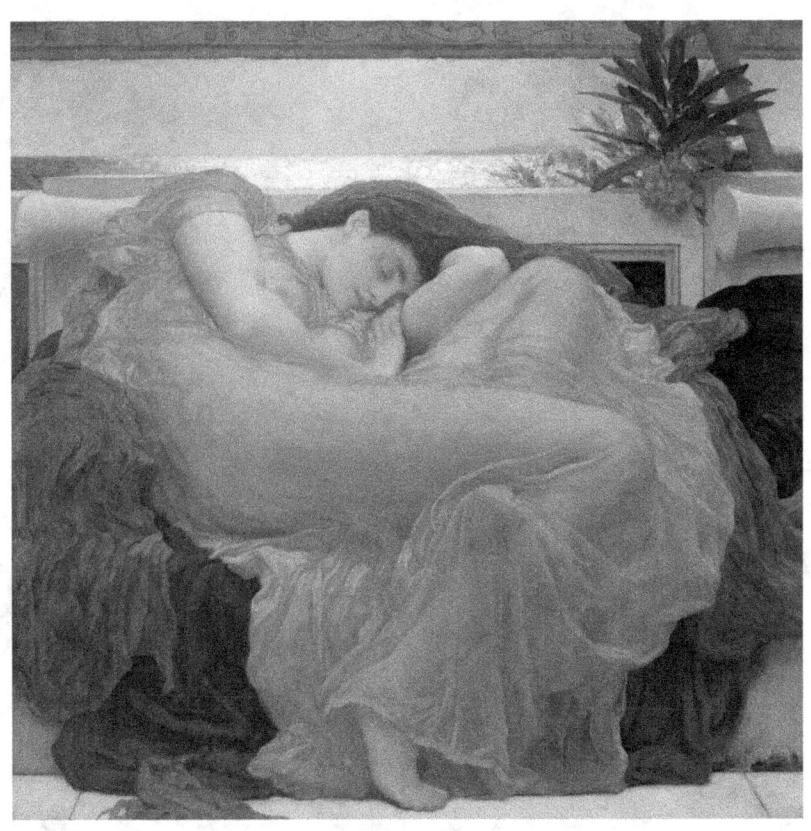

Lord Leighton, Flaming June, 1895, Puerto Rico

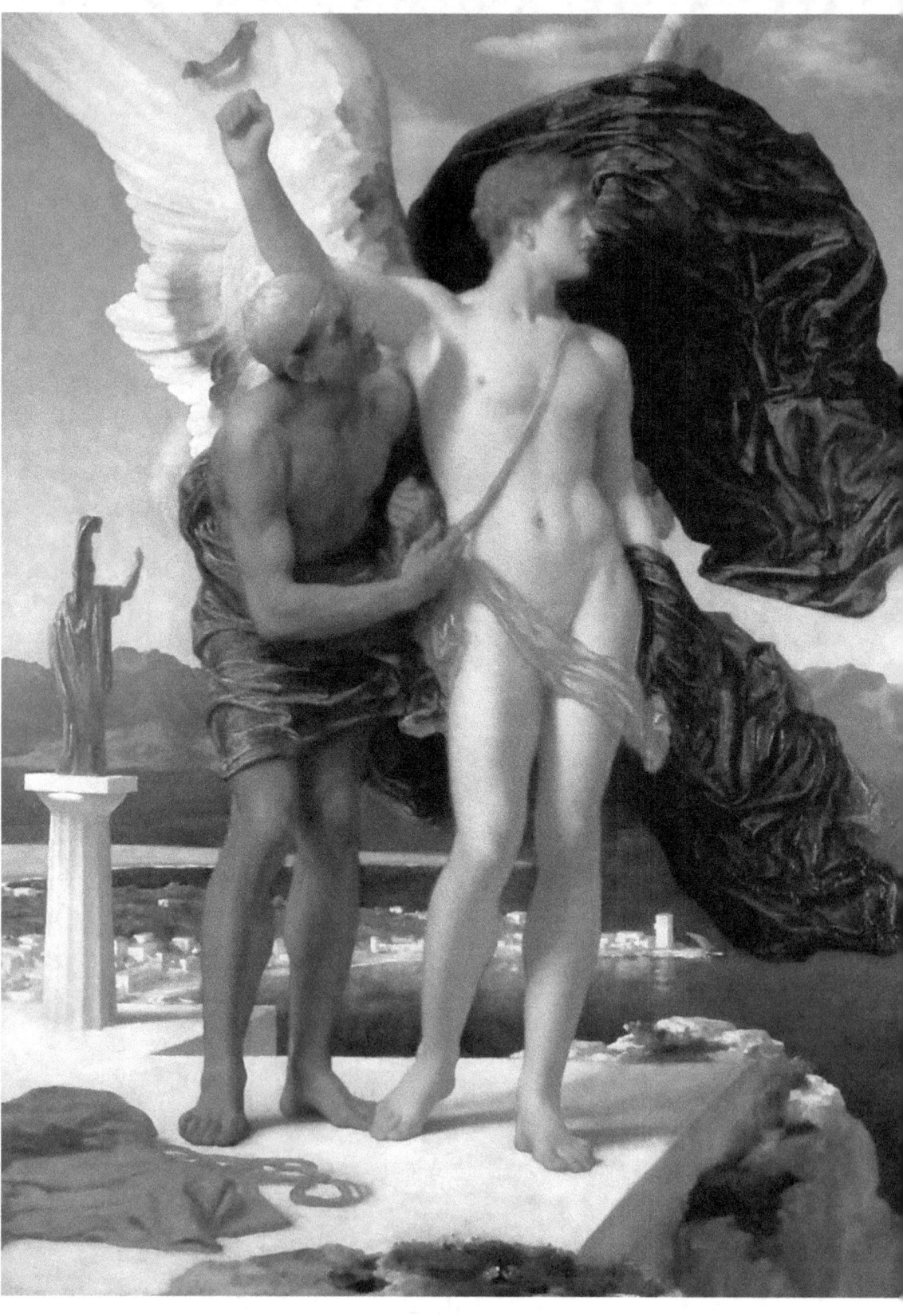

Lord Leighton, Icarus and Daedalus, 1869, private collection

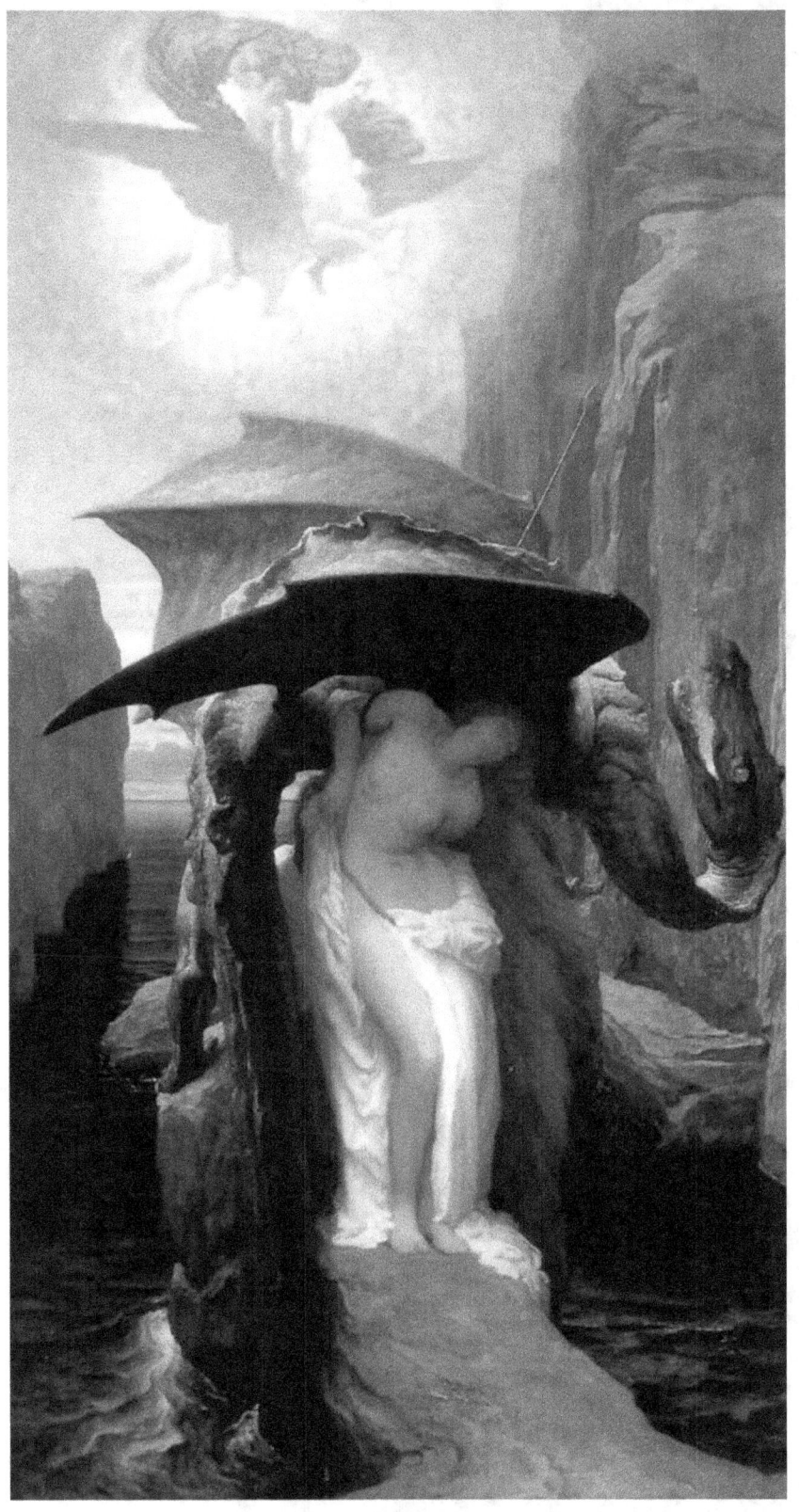

Lord Leighton, Perseus and Andromeda, 1891

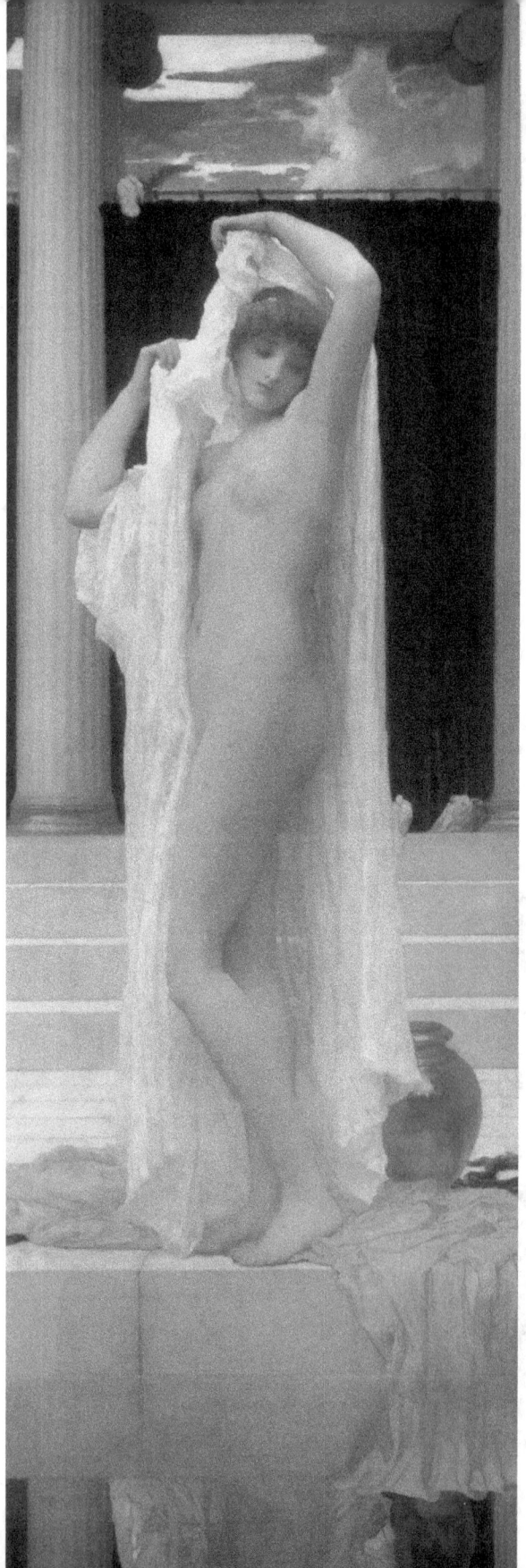

Lord Leighton,
Bath of Psyche,
1890, Tate Gallery

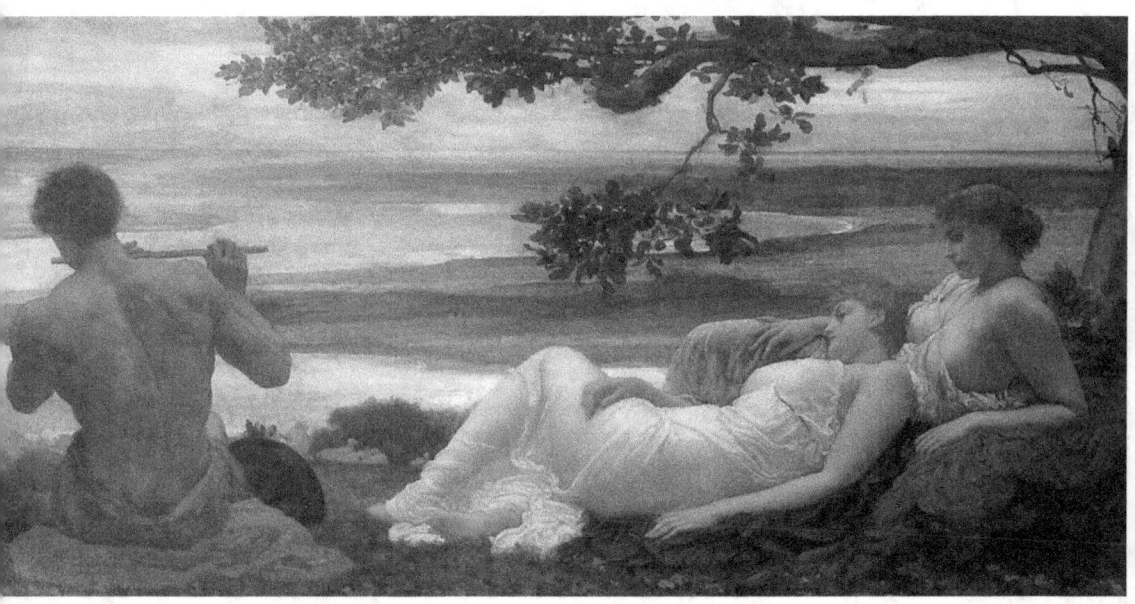

Lord Leighton, Idyll, c. 1880-81,
private collection

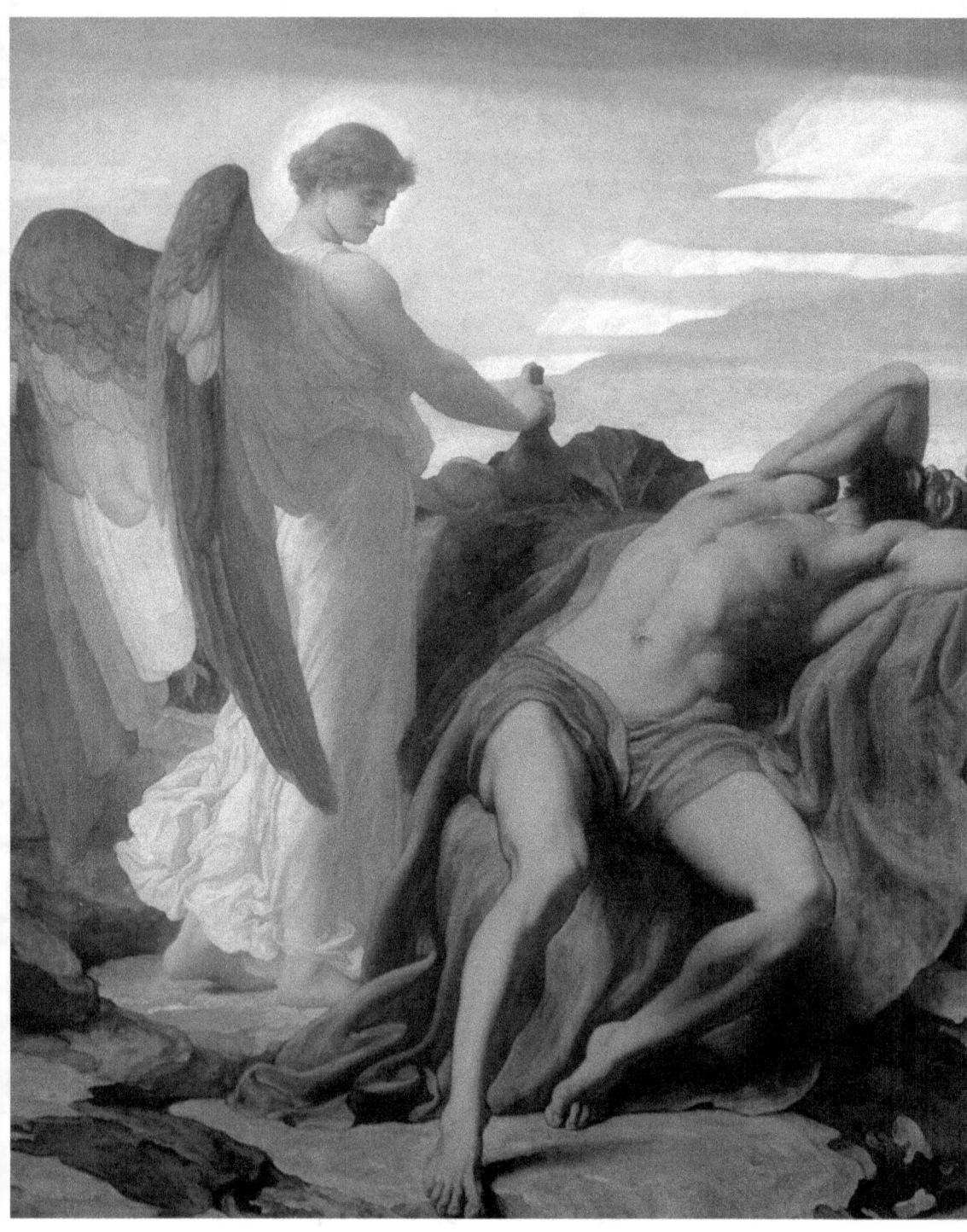

Lord Leighton, Elijah in the Wilderness, 1878, Liverpool

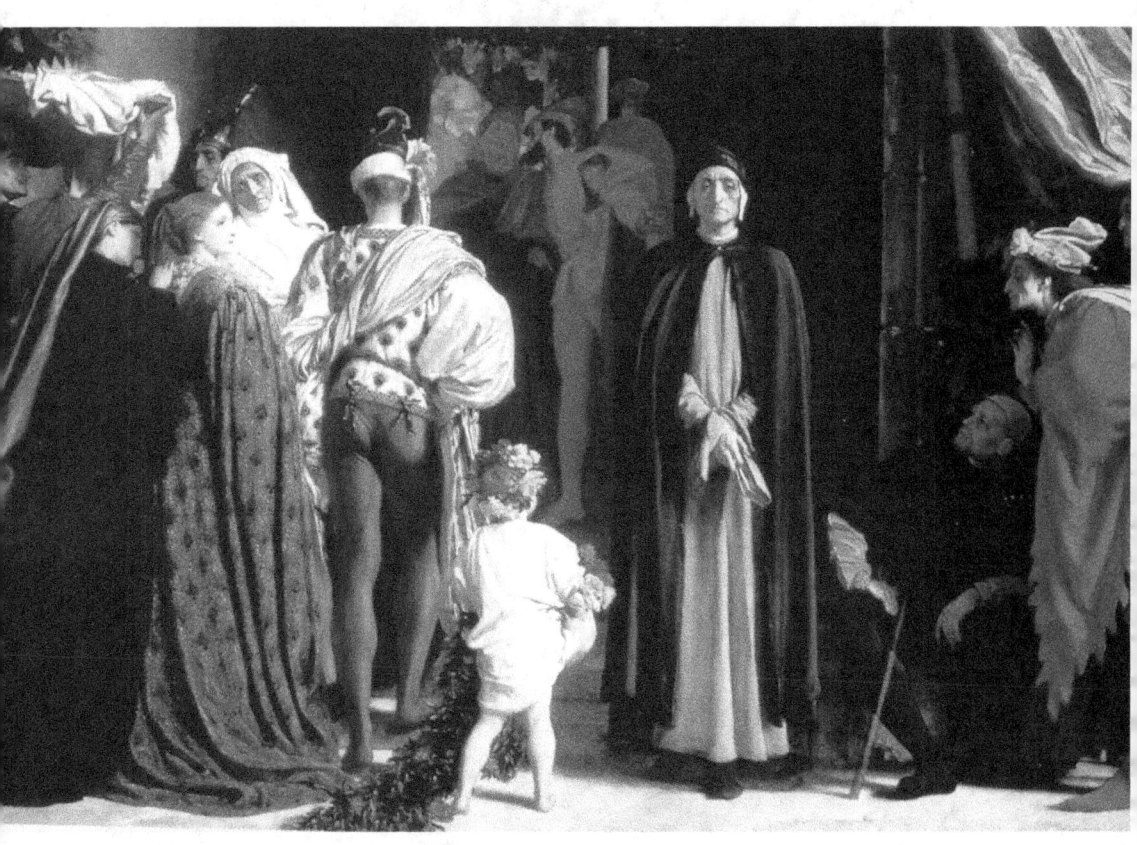

Lord Leighton, Dante In Exile, 1864, private collection

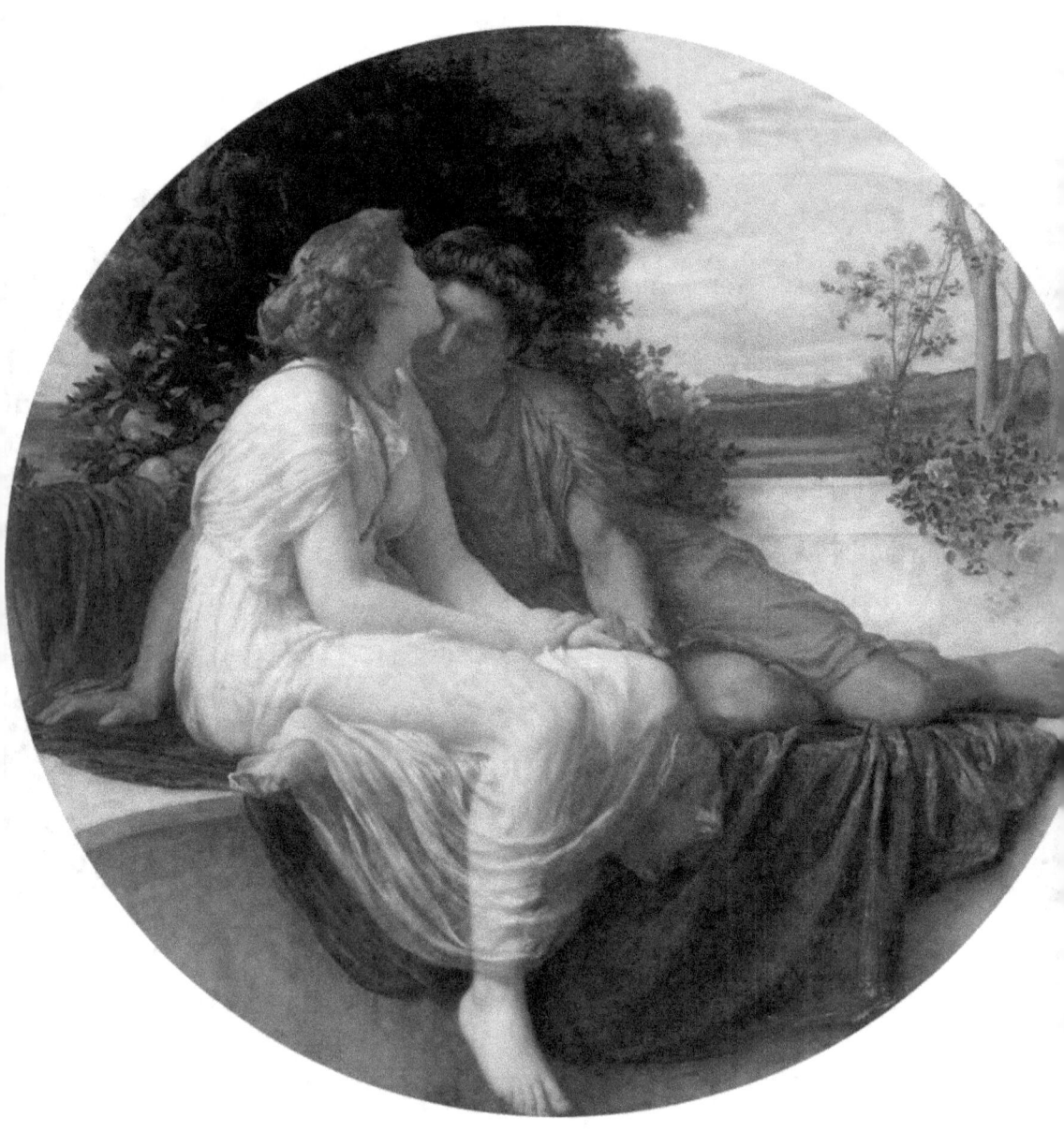

Lord Leighton, Acme and Septimius,
c. 1868, Tate Gallery

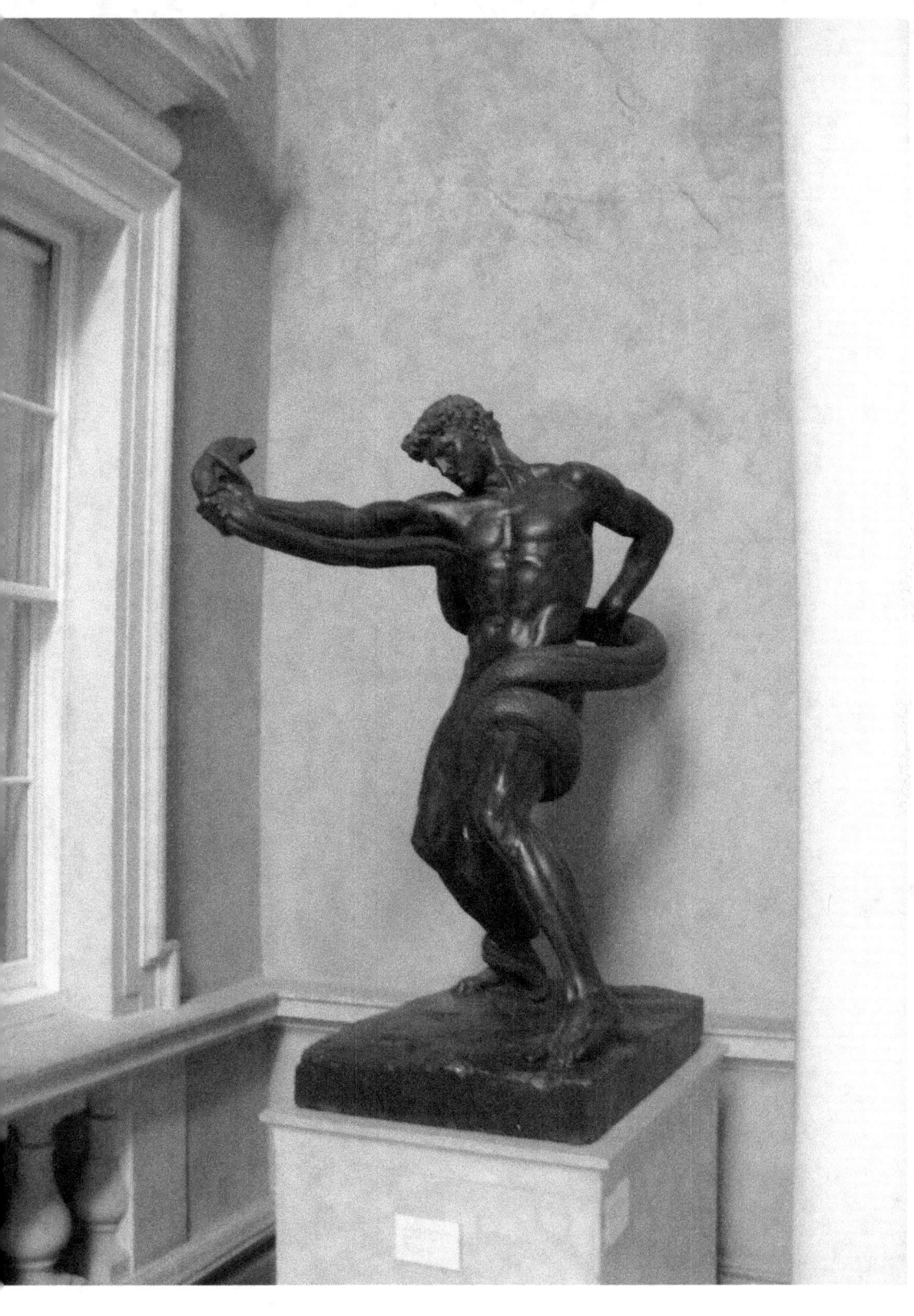

Lord Leighton, An Athlete Struggling With a Python,
1886, Royal Academy of Arts

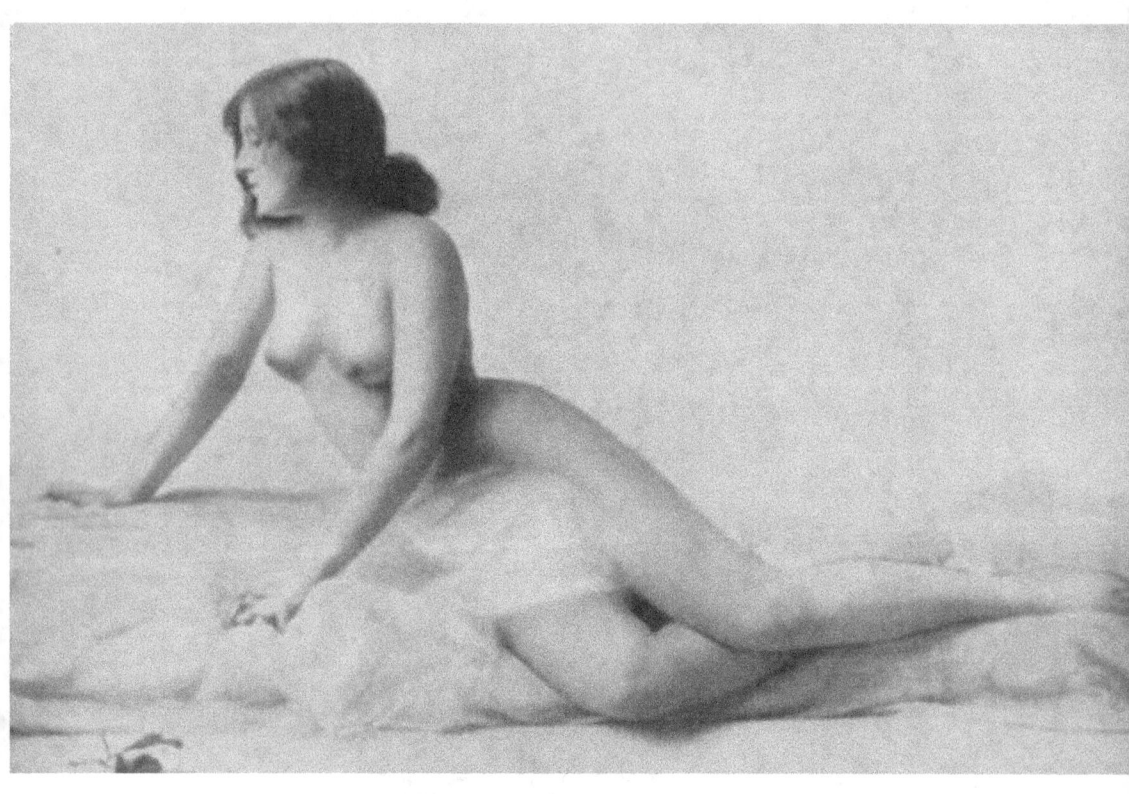

Frederick Armstrong, Greek Slave,
1909, drawn from Lord Leighton

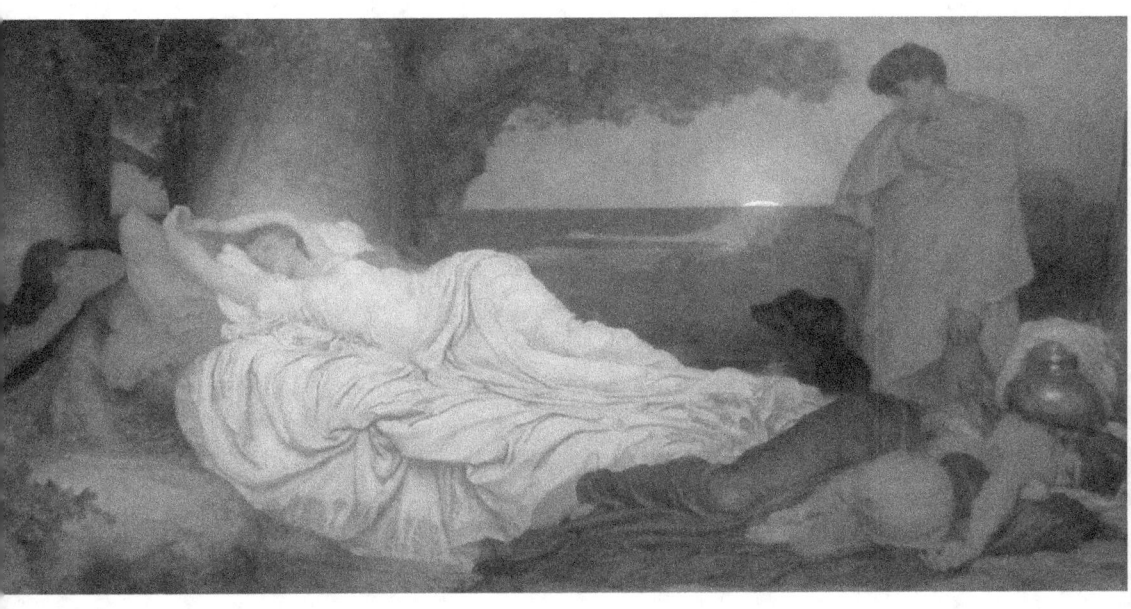

Lord Leighton, Cymon and Iphigenia, 1884, Sydney

CHAPTER V

Year by Year – 1878 to 1896

On November 13th, 1878, Frederic Leighton was elected President of the Royal Academy, in succession to Sir Francis Grant, and immediately received the honour of knighthood.

In 1879 Leighton sent eight contributions to the Academy, not one of which, with the possible exception of the *Elijah*, perhaps, has been counted among his masterpieces. Four of them belong to that group of ideal figure paintings which almost constitute a *genre* in themselves: *Biondina*, *Catarina*, *Amarilla*, and *Neruccia*, a girl with a red flower in her hair, in white dress, against a dark background. The finely austere *Elijah in the Wilderness* was an addition to the notable group of Scriptural paintings. In this picture the nude figure of the prophet is seen reclining on a rock, with head and arms thrown back, while beside him stands an angel holding bread and water. The striking and powerful *Portrait of Professor Costa*, the *Portrait of the Countess Brownlow*, and a portrait study, completed the list of the year's contributions, the largest number ever sent in by Leighton, before his election or afterward. This year ten of his landscape-studies in oil were exhibited at the Grosvenor Gallery.

It may be thought by the outsider that the coveted office of the

President of the Royal Academy of Arts is, in a way, an ornamental one, – some such golden sinecure as that of the old High Chamberlains. Nothing could be more mistaken. "Not everybody," wrote the late Mr. Underhill, who for some time, as private secretary to Sir Frederic Leighton, had special opportunities of knowing, "is aware of the tax upon a man's time and energy that is involved in the acceptance of the office in question. The post is a peculiar one, and requires a combination of talents not frequently to be found, inasmuch as it demands an established standing as a painter, together with great urbanity and considerable social position. The inroads which the occupancy of the office makes upon an artist's time are very considerable. There is, on the average, at least one Council meeting for every three weeks throughout the whole of the year. There are from time to time general assemblies for the election of new members and for other purposes, over which the President is bound, of course, to preside. For ten days or a fortnight in every April he has to be in attendance with the Council daily at Burlington House, for the purpose of selecting the pictures which are to be hung in the Spring Exhibition. He has to preside over the banquet which yearly precedes the opening of the Academy, and he has to act as host at the annual conversazione. Finally, it is his duty every other year to deliver a long, elaborate, and carefully prepared 'Discourse' upon matters connected with art, to the students who are for that purpose assembled. It is a post of much honour and small profit."

In filling this post, and neglecting no one of its smallest offices and endless small courtesies, an artist had needs be without the characteristic artist's defects of hesitation and delay; and in fact, Lord Leighton mastered, as much as any statesman of our time, the indispensable secret of despatch. We quote from Mr. Underhill again: "To administer the affairs of the Academy, to fulfil a round of social semi-public and public engagements, and to paint pictures which invariably reach a high level of excellence, would of course be impossible – even to Sir Frederic Leighton –

were it not for the fact that he makes the very most of the time at his disposal. 'That's the secret,' remarked a distinguished member of the Academy to the present writer some little time before the President's death; 'Sir Frederic knows exactly how long it will take to do a certain thing, and he apportions his time accordingly.' This being the case, no one will be surprised to learn that he attached the greatest importance to punctuality. He himself never failed to keep an appointment at the exact moment fixed upon, and he expected, of course, similar punctuality on the part of others. The stroke of eight from the Academy clock was the signal for Sir Frederic to enter the Council Room at Burlington House, and to open the deliberations of the body over which he presided. 'They will never again get a man to devote so much time and energy to the business of the Academy,' said Sir Frederic Leighton's most distinguished colleague shortly before his death; 'never again.'" And since that time the same tribute has been paid ungrudgingly in public and private often enough.

In 1880, we are tempted by five canvases; of which the *Sister's Kiss* and *Psamathe*, are perhaps the most important. The former turns a garden wall to delightful account, in its picture of a child, who is seated upon it, and of her charmingly drawn elder sister, who gives the kiss. The composition of this picture may be seen in our reproduction, but the colour of the bronze green robe – of singular beauty – is of course not even suggested. More classic, perhaps, and not less picturesque, is the Greek maiden, Psamathe, who was, if we remember aright, one of the Nereides. The artist has painted her sitting by the seashore, gazing over the Ægean, with her back turned to the spectator. Filmy garments, which have slipped from her shoulders on to the sand; arms folded about her knees; every detail of the picture carries out the effect of dreamy loveliness that pervades Psamathe and her surroundings. *Iostephane* is a three-quarter length figure, less than life size, of a girl in light yellow drapery, with violets in her fair hair, who stands facing the spectator and arranging her draperies over her right arm; there are marble columns and a fountain in the background. *The Light of the Harem* is a version of one of the groups in the fresco of *The Industrial Arts of Peace* at South Kensington. The picture now known as the *Nymph of the Dargle* was also exhibited this year under the title of *Crenaia*. It represents a small full-length figure facing the spectator; the river Dargle flows through Powerscourt, and forms the waterfall here represented in the background, hence its name. *Rubinella*, a girl with red gold hair was shown at the Summer Exhibition and a large number of sketches and studies at the Winter Exhibition of the Grosvenor Gallery this year.

In 1881, the portrait of the Painter, painted by invitation in 1880 for the collection of autograph portraits of artists in the Uffizi Gallery, Florence, deserves particular mention. Not even Mr. Watts' best portrait of Leighton is quite so like as this, which shows the striking head of the artist to great effect, assisted by the decorative President's robe and insignia. The *Idyll*, shown the same year, has been compared by some critics with the *Cymon and Iphigenia*, the scene and circumstance of both being to a certain degree similar, while there are similar effects in both of colour and of composition. In the *Idyll*, we have a lovely female figure, lying at full length, attended by a second nymph, and by a piping man, all grouped beneath an arm of a beech tree, that extends overhead and shadows the upland ridge on which they have come to rest, while they gaze on a river winding among sunlit meads. The water reflects the blue and white of sky and clouds; the land is dashed by shadows. The nymphs' robes are red, blue, and pale yellow.

We ought not to overlook another idyllic picture in the same exhibition, *Whispers*, an illustration of Horace's well-known line, "Lenesque sub noctem susurri." In this charming work, amid masses of crimson flowers and green leaves, two lovers are seen seated upon a marble bench, while he whispers tenderly in her ear, and she listens with dreamy eyes and maidenly mien. The noble picture of *Elisha and the Shunamite's Son* (reproduced at p. 114) was also shown this year, as well as *Bianca*, a fair-haired girl in a white dress, standing with folded arms, *Viola*, and two portraits, *Mrs. Augustus Ralli*, exhibited at the Royal Academy, and *Mrs. Algernon Sartoris*, at the Grosvenor Gallery.

In the 1882 Academy appeared two of the most popular of Sir Frederic's pictures, *Wedded* and *Day Dreams*. In the latter, a fair Sybarite is pressing her cheek against her hands, as she stands near a tapestry, with eyes gazing far away, the images of love-dreams in them; her purple mantle, embroidered with silver, produces a charming effect of colour. Still more famous is *Wedded*, – "one of the happiest of Sir Frederic's designs," said a critic at the time, "and as a composition of lines, difficult, subtle, and original, may be called one of the most remarkable productions of this decade." Other pictures shown this year were *Antigone* and the much-debated *Phryne at Eleusis* – a notable study of the famous hetaira, who is seen standing, and holding out with one hand the mass of her deep auburn hair. Her skin is of a ruddy golden hue, as if seen under a glow of sunlight. Red tissue, which falls from her shoulders and extended arms, and an olive-coloured mantle that has fallen at the foot of the marble columns behind her, backed by a sky, very characteristic of the painter, in which snowlike masses of cloud float in a southern azure, produce a total effect of a certain super-womanly order of beauty. A *Design for a portion of a Proposed Decoration in St. Paul's*, a picture entitled *Melittion*, and a *Portrait of Mrs. Mocatta*, were also hung at the Academy in 1882; *Zeyra*, a little Eastern child in plum coloured headdress, a rich bit of colour elaborately painted, was shown at the Grosvenor Gallery.

In 1883, *Memories*, though not one of the most typical of Leighton's pictures, decidedly pleased the general public. It shows the half-length figure of a blonde, in a black and gold dress. More interesting artistically was a decorative frieze, *The Dance*, for a drawing-room, the design for which we reproduce, and which may, in so far, answer for itself. Other pictures of 1883 are *Kittens*, a full-length figure of a fair-haired child in purple and embroidered drapery, seated on a bench covered with a leopard skin, holding a rose in hand and looking down at a kitten sitting beside her; and the *Vestal*, a bust of a girl with her head and shoulders swathed with white gold-embroidered draperies. To this year also belongs a *Portrait of Miss Nina Joachim*, a child in a blue frock with crimson sash.

The next year, 1884, brought *Letty*, that most delightful of English maidens, *A Nap*, *Sun Gleams*, and the imaginative and admirably romantic *Cymon and Iphigenia*. *Letty* was one of Leighton's pictures which particularly excited Mr. Ruskin's admiration. It shows a simply pretty child, with soft brown hair under a black hat, a saffron kerchief about her neck. The *Letty* and the *Cymon and Iphigenia*, with a few other notable pictures, did much to leave a pleasant recollection of the exceptional Academy of 1884. "A more original effect of light and colour, used in the broad, true, and ideal treatment of lovely forms," said a French critic, "we do not remember to have seen at the Academy, than that produced by the *Cymon and Iphigenia*." Engravings and other reproductions of the picture have made its design, at any rate, almost as familiar now as Boccaccio's tale itself. There are some divergences, however, in the two versions. Boccaccio's tale is a tale of spring; Sir Frederic, the better to carry out his conception of the drowsy desuetude of sleep, and of that sense of pleasant but absolute weariness which one associates with the season of hot days and short nights, has changed the spring into that riper summer-time which is on the verge of autumn; and that hour of late sunset which is on the verge of night. Under its rich glow lies the sleeping Iphigenia, draped in folds upon folds of white, and her attendants; while Cymon, who is as unlike the boor of tradition as Spenser's Colin Clout is unlike an ordinary Cumbrian herdsman, stands hard-by, wondering, pensively wrapt in so exquisite a vision. Altogether, a great presentment of an immortal idyll; so treated, indeed, that it becomes much more than a mere reading of Boccaccio, and gives an ideal picture of Sleep itself, – that Sleep which so many artists and poets have tried at one time or another to render.

In 1885, among the five contributions of the President to the Academy, appeared the vivacious portrait of Lord Rosebery's little daughter, *The Lady Sybil Primrose*, who appears in white with a blue sash, carrying a doll. *A Portrait of Mrs. A. Hichens* and *Phœbe* were the only other pictures this year. A frieze, *Music*, was shown, and at the Grosvenor Gallery *A Study* of a fair-haired girl, in green velvet dress. 1886 was chiefly notable for the statue in bronze of *The Sluggard*, in which Leighton again furnished us with a plastic characterization of Sleep, which he designed by way of contrast to his statue of the struggling Athlete. It was suggested, Mr. Spielmann says, by accidental circumstances. The model who had been sitting to him fell a-yawning in his interval of rest, and charmed the artist, not only with his exceptional beauty of line and play of muscle, but also with the artistic contrast of energy and languor. But that he might not lay himself open to the charge that the work was a glorification of indolence, the sculptor made concession to what after all was an artistic suggestion, and placed under the yawner's foot

"The glorious wreath of laurel leaves
Heel trodden and despised."

The graceful statuette of a little girl who is alarmed by a toad on the edge of a pool or stream of water, called *Needless Alarms*, appeared at the same time; and was so much admired by the President's colleague, Sir John Everett Millais, that he wished to purchase it, whereupon Sir Frederic presented it to him, and received, in return, the charming picture of *Shelling Peas*, which Sir John painted specially for this pleasant exchange. In 1886 also appeared the *Decoration in Painting for a Music Room*, destined for New York, which is illustrated[7] by the completed work, and its preliminary studies from life for it. *Gulnihal*, a single figure, is the only other painting exhibited at the Academy in this year.

In 1887 appeared a picture which seems scarcely to have received its due appreciation, *The Jealousy of Simætha the Sorceress*. This is a seated figure in yellow and white drapery, with a purple mantle wrapped around her shoulders; a well-wrought, finely-rendered work. *The Last Watch of Hero,* also first seen this year, is now in the Manchester Corporation Gallery. It is in two compartments; in the upper, and larger, Hero, clad in pink drapery, is seen drawing aside a curtain and gazing out over the sea. Below, in the smaller panel, is the body of the dead Leander, on a rock washed by the waves. A quotation from Sir Edwin Arnold's translation of Musæus was appended to its title:

> "With aching heart she scanned the sea-face dim.
> • • • •
> Lo! at the turret's foot his body lay,
> Rolled on the stones and washed with breaking spray."

A picture of a little girl with yellow hair and pale blue eyes, entitled with a verse by Robert Browning:

> "Yellow and pale as ripened corn
> Which Autumn's kiss frees, – grain from sheath, –
> Such was her hair, while her eyes beneath
> Showed Spring's faint violets freshly born,"

was in the same exhibition, and also a design for the reverse of the Jubilee medallion, executed for her Majesty's Government.

In 1888 appeared another large work, which, although not absolutely a procession, has much in common with the *Cimabue,* the *Syracusan Bride,* and *The Daphnephoria.* It was entitled *Captive Andromache,* and accompanied by a fragment of the "Iliad," translated by E. B. Browning:

> ... "Some standing by
> Marking thy tears fall, shall say, 'This is she,
> The wife of that same Hector that fought best
> Of all the Trojans when all fought for Troy.'"

This, and a *Portrait of Amy, Lady Coleridge,* were the artist's only contributions to the Royal Academy of 1888. The *Portraits of the Misses Stewart Hodgson* is also of this year, which saw four landscape studies exhibited at the Royal Society of Painters in Water Colours, and five at the Royal Society of British Artists, Suffolk Street.

The *Sibyl*, exhibited in 1889, is a full-length figure swathed in lilac drapery, seated with her legs crossed, on a chair, her chin supported by her left hand, and gazing out of the picture. Beside her are scrolls, and a sombre sky is behind the figure. *Invocation*, a girl in white robes with arms raised above her head, and a *Portrait of Mrs. F. Lucas*, were also shown; but *Greek Girls playing at Ball* is not only the most important, but is also a picture that shows the mannerism of Lord Leighton's treatment of drapery at its finest. Elsewhere the undulating snaky coils may be somewhat distressing, here they float in the air and help the suggestion of movement. The landscape at the back is also both typical and beautiful. An *Elegy* was the fifth of the artist's contributions to the Academy of 1889.

In 1890 *The Bath of Psyche* appeared at the Academy. This at once established its position as a popular favourite, and has probably been more widely reproduced than any other. It was purchased under the terms of the Chantrey Bequest, and is now in the Tate Gallery. It was suggested, so Mr. M. H. Spielmann tells us, by the "paper-knife" picture, as Lord Leighton called it, which he had painted for Sir L. Alma-Tadema's wall screen. *Solitude* was also shown this year, and the *Tragic Poetess*, a full-length figure, clad in blue and purple drapery, on a terrace, with the sea beyond. The fourth picture at the Academy was a very faithfully painted transcript of *The Arab Hall*, at No. 2, Holland Park Road.

In 1891 appeared *Perseus and Andromeda*, a very original version of a theme which it seems the destiny of every painter and sculptor of classical subjects to attempt at some time. In this Andromeda is bound to a rock, the monster stands over her with outstretched wings, while from the clouds above, Perseus, on his winged steed, is discharging arrows. The clay models for Perseus are reproduced elsewhere (at p. 68). The *Return of Persephone* was another important work shown this year. It represents Persephone, supported by Hermes, being brought back to the upper world, where she is awaited with outstretched arms by Demeter. A *Portrait of A. B. Mitford, Esq.*, and a marble version of the *Athlete Struggling with a Python*, were also shown in the same exhibition.

In 1892 a version of a panel of the proposed decoration for the dome of St. Paul's appeared with the title, *And the Sea gave up the Dead which were in it*; this, purchased by Mr. Henry Tate, is now among the pictures he gave to the Gallery at Millbank. The most important of Leighton's later works, *The Garden of the Hesperides*, in many respects the most sumptuous piece of decoration he ever achieved, was shown this year. It is a large circular picture, the centre occupied by a tree bearing golden apples; under its branches recline the three Hesperides, caressing the dragon who assists them to guard the treasure. A superbly brilliant sea is in the distance. The charm of this picture is mainly in its colour, but as an example of elaborately artificial composition it is hardly less noteworthy. Unfortunately, despite every effort of Lord Leighton, most kindly exerted on behalf of the editor of this volume, the owners of the copyright refused under any condition to allow it to be illustrated herein. *A Bacchante*, and *At the Fountain*, a girl in fawn-coloured and violet draperies, with a bunch of lemons overhanging the marble wall behind her, were shown this year; and also a *Clytie*, which must not be confused with another known by the same title, the last picture on which the artist was at work before his death. The 1892 version, shown in the retrospective exhibition, is thus described in its catalogue: "A small figure of Clytie is seen on the right, kneeling on a stone building with arms outstretched towards the sun, which is setting behind a range of moorland hills."

In 1893 *Hit, The Frigidarium, Farewell, Corinna of Tanagra*, and *Rizpah* were exhibited at the Academy. Of these the most important is the last named. It illustrates the story of the two sons of Rizpah, by Saul, Armoni and Mephibosheth, who were slain by the Gideonites. Rizpah, robed in dark blue, is seen in the act of fetching away their bodies, which are shrouded by dull lilac and blue draperies. Vultures circle above, and two leopards approach stealthily. *Farewell* is a single figure in olive green and plum-coloured peplis under a portico above the sea, where she pauses to take a last look at an outward-bound ship.

Atalanta depicts the bust only of a dark-haired girl in purple and white drapery, with a snake-like ornament twisted round her arm, which is bare to the shoulder. *Corinna of Tanagra* is a half-length figure crowned with leaves, in coloured drapery, resting her clasped hands upon her lyre. *The Frigidarium* is an upright figure in semi-transparent red drapery, which with the background of gold is reflected in the water beneath her feet.

In 1894 were shown *The Spirit of the Summit*, a white-robed figure with upturned face, sitting on a snowy peak, with starlit sky beyond; *The Bracelet*; *Fatidica*, a figure in green-white robes; *At the Window*, a dark-haired boy in blue, looking over the ledge of a window; and *Summer Slumber*. This last is a somewhat elaborate composition; a girl in salmon colour draperies is lying asleep on the broad rim of a marble fountain, masses of flowers are in the mid distance, and a vista of sunny landscape through the open window beyond.

In 1895, the last year of the artist's working life, he sent six pictures to the Academy, and completed the wall decoration at the Royal Exchange (here illustrated), *Phœnicians Bartering with Britons*. The paintings were entitled, *Flaming June* (a picture reproduced in colours for a Christmas number of the "Graphic"), in which the "broad" painting of the sea beyond was a notable exception to the artist's usual handling; *Lachrymæ*, a standing figure in robes of black and blue green, resting her arm upon a Doric column; *'Twixt Hope and Fear*, a seated figure of a black-haired Greek girl, robed in white and olive, with a sheep-skin thrown around her; *The Maid with her Yellow Hair*, a girlish figure in lemon-coloured drapery, reading from a red-backed book; *Listener*, a child seated with crossed legs on a fur rug; and a *Study of a Girl's Head*, with auburn, wavy hair.

In the 1896 Academy *Clytie* was the only picture. In Lord Leighton's studio in various stages of completion were a *Bacchante*, a half-length figure of a fair-haired girl crowned with leaves, and a leopard skin over her shoulder; *The Fair Persian*, a bust of a girl with flowing dark hair, crowned by a jewelled circlet; and *The Vestal*, a half-length figure of a girl in white drapery, these were all exhibited at the Winter Exhibition of 1897.

To *Clytie*, his last picture, a small monograph has been devoted by the Fine Art Society. In this we read:

> "'Thank goodness my ailment has not interfered with my capacity for work, for I have never had a better appetite for it, nor I believe done better. I was idle for five months in the summer, but since my return I have been working hard and have produced the pictures you see.' Thus he spoke to the present writer [of the monograph in question] as he led the way across his studio... Turning to the *Clytie* he continued: 'This I have been at work upon all the morning. Orchardson has been so good as to say I have never done anything finer than the sky. You know the story. I have shown the goddess in adoration before the setting sun, whose last rays are permeating her whole being. With upraised arms she is entreating her beloved one not to forsake her. A flood of golden light saturates the scene, and to carry out my intention, I have changed my model's hair from black to auburn. To the right is a small altar, upon which is an offering of fruit, and upon a pillar beyond I shall show the feet of a statue of Apollo.'
>
> "But a few days after this occurrence the dead President lay in semi-state in his coffin, before the picture. A drawing in the 'Graphic' (January 26th, 1896) shows the interior of the studio, with the figure of Clytie, in her attitude of despair, stretching her arms above the body of her creator."

Here the record, year by year, is closed. A few pictures seem to have escaped the honours of exhibition. One,[8] *A Noble Lady of Venice*, in possession of Lord Armstrong, does not appear to have been exhibited. It is probably the picture which was sold at Christie's in 1875 for 950 guineas. A *Lady with Pomegranates*, which sold for 765 guineas at the sale of Baron Grant's pictures in 1877, does not appear in our list of exhibited works; nor, it may be, are

all the early pictures included therein. But the official catalogues
of the Royal Academy May Exhibitions, and of the special Winter
Exhibition devoted to the artist's works, have been freely drawn
upon for description, and to the list of his life's work, as it
appeared in the first edition of this work, many additions have
been made.

CHAPTER VI

His Method of Painting

For particulars of the wonderfully thorough "method," which Leighton used in preparing his pictures, we cannot do better than quote the following admirable account by Mr. M. H. Spielmann (published during the painter's life), which he has allowed us to reprint here. [9]

"I have said that the sense of line in composition, in figure and drapery, is one of the chief qualities of the artist; and the conviction that the method in which he places them upon canvas with such unerring success – for it may be said that the President rarely, if ever, produces an ugly form in a picture – would be both interesting and instructive, prompted me to learn in what manner his effects are produced. This I have done, having special regard to one of his Academy pictures, *The Sibyl*, which, being a single figure, simplifies greatly the explanation of the mode of procedure. This explanation holds good in every case, be the composition great or small, elaborate or simple; the *modus operandi* is always the same.

"Having by good fortune observed in a model an extraordinarily fine and 'Michelangelesque' formation of the hand and wrist – an articulation as rare to find as it is anatomically beautiful and desirable – he bethought him of a subject that would enable him to introduce his *trouvaille*. As but one attitude could display the special formation to advantage, the idea of a Sibyl, sitting brooding beside her oracular tripod, was soon evolved, but not so soon was its form determined and fixed. Like Mr. Watts, Sir Frederic Leighton thinks out the whole picture before he puts brush to canvas, or chalk to paper; but, unlike Mr. Watts, once he is decided upon his scheme of colour, the arrangement of line, the disposition of the folds, down to the minutest details, he seldom, if ever, alters a single line. And the reason is evident. In Sir Frederic's pictures – which are, above all, decorations in the real sense of the word – the design is a pattern in which every line has its place and its proper relation to other lines, so that the disturbing of one of them, outside of certain limits, would throw the whole out of gear. Having thus determined his picture in his mind's eye, he in the majority of cases makes a sketch in black and white chalk upon brown paper to fix it. In the first sketch, the care with which the folds have been broadly arranged will be evident, and, if it be compared with the finished picture, the very slight degree in which the general scheme has been departed from will convince the reader of the almost scientific precision of the artist's line of action. But there is a good reason for this determining of the draperies before the model is called in; and it is this. The nude model, no matter how practised he or she may be, never moves or stands or sits, in these degenerate days, with exactly the same freedom as when draped; action or pose is always different – not so much from a sense of mental constraint as from the unusual liberty experienced by the limbs, to which the muscular action invariably responds when the body is released from the discipline and confinement of clothing.

"The picture having been thus determined, the model is called in, and is posed as nearly as possible in the attitude desired. As nearly as possible I say, for, as no two faces are exactly alike, no two models ever entirely resemble one another in body or muscular action, and cannot, therefore, pose in such a manner as exactly to correspond with either another model or another figure – no matter how correctly the latter may be drawn. From the model the artist makes the careful outline, in brown paper, a true transcript from life, which may entail some slight corrections of the original design in the direction of modifying the attitude and general appearance of the figure. This would be rendered necessary, probably by the bulk and material of the drapery. So far, of course, the artist's attention is engaged exclusively by 'form,' 'colour' being always treated more or less ideally. The figure is now placed in its surroundings, and established in exact relation to the canvas. The result is the first true sketch of the entire design, figure and background, and is built up of the two previous ones. It must be absolutely accurate in the distribution of spaces, for it has subsequently to be 'squared off' on to the canvas, which is ordered to the exact scale of the sketch. At this moment, the design being finally determined, the sketch in oil colours is made. It has been deferred till now, because the placing of the colours is, of course, of as much importance as the harmony. This done, the canvas is for the first time produced, and thereon is enlarged the design, the painter re-drawing the outline – never departing a hair's breadth from the outlines and forms already obtained – and then highly finishing the whole figure in warm monochrome from the life. Every muscle, every joint, every crease is there, although all this careful painting is shortly to be hidden with the draperies; such, however, is the only method of insuring absolute correctness of drawing. The fourth stage completed, the artist returns once more to his brown paper, re-copies the outline accurately from the picture, on a larger scale than before, and resumes his studies of draperies in greater detail and with still greater precision, dealing with them in sections, as parts of a homogeneous whole. The draperies are now laid with infinite care on to the living model, and are made to approximate as closely as possible to the arrangement given in the first sketch, which, as it was not haphazard, but most carefully worked out, must of necessity be adhered to. They have often to be drawn piecemeal, as a model cannot by any means always retain the attitude sufficiently long for the design to be wholly carried out at one cast. This arrangement is effected with special reference to painting – that is to say, giving not only form and light and shade, but also the relation and 'values' of tones. The draperies are drawn over, and are made to conform exactly to the forms copied from the nudes of the underpainted picture. This is a cardinal point, because in carrying out the picture the folds are found fitting mathematically on to the nude, or nudes, first established on the canvas. The next step then is to transfer these draperies to the canvas on which the design has been squared off, and this is done with flowing colour in the same monochrome as before over the nudes, to which they are intelligently applied, and which nudes must never – mentally at least – be lost sight of. The canvas has been prepared with a grey tone, lighter or darker, according to the subject in hand, and the effect to be produced. The background and accessories being now added, the whole picture presents a more or less completed aspect – resembling that, say, of a print of any warm tone. In the case of draperies of very vigorous tone, a rich flat local colour is probably rubbed over them, the modelling underneath being, though thin, so sharp and definite as to assert itself through this wash. Certain portions of the picture might probably be prepared with a wash or flat tinting of a colour the *opposite* of that which it is eventually to receive. A blue sky, for instance, would possibly have a soft, ruddy tone spread over the canvas – the sky, which is a very definite and important part of the President's compositions, being as completely drawn in monochrome as any other portion of the design; or for rich blue mountains a strong orange wash or tint might be used as a bed. The structure of the picture being thus absolutely complete, and the effect distinctly determined by a sketch which it is the painter's aim to equal in the big work, he has nothing to think of but colour, and with that he now proceeds deliberately, but rapidly.

"Such is the method by which Sir Frederic Leighton finds it convenient to build up his pictures. The labour entailed by such a system as this is, of course, enormous, more especially when the composition to be worked out is of so complex a character as the *Captive Andromache* of last year, every figure and group of which were treated with the same completeness and detail as we have seen to attend the production of so simple a picture as *The Sibyl*. Deliberateness of workmanship and calculation of effect, into which inspiration of the moment is never allowed to enter, are the chief characteristics of the painter's craftsmanship. The inspiration stage was practically passed when he took the crayon in his hand; and to this circumstance probably is to be assigned the absence of realism which arrests the attention of the beholder."

Mr. Spielmann has instanced, in the above account, the tragic and lovely *Captive Andromache*, exhibited in 1888; and we may further add that exquisite painting of *Greek Girls playing at Ball*, of 1889; or the still more exquisite *Bath of Psyche*, of the year following. All three are full of technical delicacy and finesse. For other qualities take that radiantly pictured myth, the *Perseus and Andromeda*, or the *Return of Persephone* (both of 1891); or the lovely *Clytie* of 1892, whose sunset background was painted at Malinmore, on the west coast of Donegal; or the *Atalanta* or the *Rizpah* of 1893.

The memorable picture, first named of these, which shows Andromache at the Well, is in particular a most characteristic example of the artist's larger style. In it, true to his classic predilections, he gives a new setting to the touching old story of Andromache's captivity. Following up the earlier scene in the "Iliad," where Andromache begs her husband Hector not to sally forth to battle, but to stay and defend the city, and where, finding her prayers in vain, and weeping, she bids Hector farewell, the picture shows the fulfilment of Andromache's fears and the dire prophecy which Hector had recalled to his wife.

By way of contrast to this sombre canvas, take the glowing and brilliant colours of the *Perseus and Andromeda*, one of the three pictures shown at the Academy in 1891. The painting of the surroundings of Andromeda, the deep blue water in the sea lagoon beneath, and these radiant elemental people of air and light, provides such a glow of colour, as haunts the eye for long after one has gazed one's fill upon it. Something of the same feeling for the spirit that is in the forces of the earth, lurks behind many of Leighton's representments of the classic myths. It is certainly to be found, with a difference, in the *Return of Persephone*, exhibited with the *Perseus*, which becomes in the artist's hands a profound allegory of the return of Spring, with all kind of symbolical meanings in the three figures of Proserpine, Ceres, and Hermes, that are seen meeting before the mouth of Hades. *The Spirit of the Summit*, one of the latest of these embodiments of the relation of Man to Nature, may be read to mean Man's finer spirit of aspiration, and the mountainous imagination of Art itself. It is characteristic of the artist that, in the later years of his career, at a time when most artists and men are apt to give up something of their earlier pursuit of ideals, he retained undiminished a feeling for the unaccomplished heights of the imagination. *The Spirit of the Summit* may serve, then, as the symbol, not so much of things attained, and Art victorious, as of things that are always to be attained, and of Art striving and undeterred. In this way it may serve, too, as in some sort the emblem of Leighton's own ideals, and of his whole career. His artistic temper was throughout, one of endless energy, endless determination; with a dash of that finer dissatisfaction which is always seeking out new embodiments, under all difficulties, of Man's pursuit, in a difficult, and often an unbeautiful world, of Truth and Beauty. Above all, he was a consummate draughts-man, and as Francisco Pacheco, the father-in-law of Velasquez, wrote in his "Arte de la Pintura" (1649): "Drawing is the life and soul of painting; drawing, especially outline, is the hardest; nay, the Art has, strictly speaking, no other difficulty. Without drawing painting is nothing but a vulgar craft; those who neglect it are bastards of the Art, mere daubers and blotchers."

CHAPTER VII

MURAL DECORATION, SCULPTURE, AND ILLUSTRATION

The drawings of Lord Leighton deserve special consideration. The famous *Lemon Tree* was made at Capri in the Spring of 1859; it is work that no Pre-Raphaelite could have finished more minutely, yet it has nothing "niggling" in its treatment. In a conversation [10] Lord Leighton is said to have referred to the many days spent upon the production of this study – dwelling specially on the difficulty he experienced in finding again and again each separate leaf in the perspective of the confused branches, as morning after morning he returned at sunrise to continue the work. The drawing of each leaf reveals the close observation which ultimately recorded its particular individuality. You feel that as a shepherd knows his sheep to call each by its name, so the artist must have become familiar with every separate leaf and twig before he had completed his task. The whole is broad and simple, and scarcely suggests the enormous patience which must have been needed to carry out the self-imposed toil. Nothing is shirked, nothing is scamped; from the stem to the outermost leaf, every part in succession reveals equal interest, and yet the whole is not without that larger quality which brings it together in a harmonious whole, so that it is as much the study of a tree as the study of each separate item that composes it.

The *Byzantine Well-head* is another notable instance of similar labour devoted to an architectural subject; this was evidently a favourite with its author; for during his life it hung close by his bed in the simple chamber of his otherwise sumptuous home, a room devoid of luxury and almost ascetic in its appointments. [11]

The great mass of studies, on brown paper chiefly, which he had carefully preserved, were purchased by the Fine Art Society, and some two hundred and fifty were exhibited at their gallery in December, 1896, and a selection in facsimile has been published in sumptuous form. In a prefatory note to the catalogue of these studies Mr. S. Pepys Cockerell says:

"It is seldom that we are privileged to watch at ease the workings of another's mind, but these drawings, the intimate record of a long life-time, offer an unusually good opportunity. One might call them the confessions of an artist; and anyone who wants to know what Leighton was really like, has only to use his eyes. One thing, at any rate, no one can fail to see, viz., that he had the qualities which result in industry. Whatever success he achieved was only gained after desperate labour. It is curious that while he had the reputation for working with ease, he considered himself to have no facility for anything, whether for art, for writing, or for speaking. I recollect his once saying: 'Thank Heaven, I was never clever at anything,' for he believed with Sir Joshua, that everything is granted to well-deserved labour."

The landscape studies in oil (of which a list almost complete will be found in Appendix II.), show equal observation and sympathetic perception of the beauty of colour, as well as of the beauty of form. The truth of these carefully recorded impressions of scenery was no less patent than the masterly "selection" which had set itself to depict all that seemed of value, and escaped at once the photographic imitation of one school, and the evasion of detail of another. They all preserve a certain classic repose, without violence to topographical accuracy, or painter-like intention.

We have had occasion to refer frequently, in passing, to Leighton's decorative works, but we have purposely deferred any description of them, preferring to treat them separately. To know how present was his feeling for decorative effect at all times, it is sufficient to glance never so casually at his own house, about which we hope presently to say something, – genuine expression as it is of his Art. Now we wish rather to touch on his more public performances. Of these, the famous frescoes which fill large lunettes in the central court at South Kensington, *The Industrial Arts of War* and *The Industrial Arts of Peace*, are the best known, as they are among the most characteristic of all the artist's productions.

The fresco of *The Arts of War* is a very complex piece of work. It is crowded with figures, full of that orderly disorder which one must expect to find, on the hurried morning of a day of battle, in these delightfully decorative warriors. "In the centre" – we quote here Mrs. Lang's description – "is a white marble staircase, leading from the quadrangle to an archway, beyond which is another courtyard. Seen through the archway, knights are riding by... The busy scene in the courtyard suggests an immediate departure to the seat of war. In the corner to the right crossbows are being chosen and tested; a man is kneeling by a pile of swords, and descanting on their various merits to an undecided customer, while those weapons that he has already disposed of are having their blades tried and felt. A little way off, to the left of the archway, some men-at-arms are trying on the armour of a youth who has still to win his spurs... The whole is distinguished by the extreme naturalness and simplicity of all the actions, and by soft, glowing colours, chiefly dark olive green and splendid saffrons."

In *The Arts of Peace*, its companion, the central portion of the fresco is devised as the interior of a Greek house, where within a semicircular alcove we see a number of Greek maidens and older women, delightfully grouped, mainly occupied in the art of personal adornment. Before this house is the waterside, with a very decorative boat, confined by a gracefully-looped chain, whose curve, as it hangs, is very subtly designed to complete the salient lines of the whole composition. On either side of this interior we have groups of men, more vigorously treated, – drawing water, bearing burdens, pushing a boat from land. The total effect of these finely posed contrasted groups, of the admirably architectured walls, piers, and pavements, and of the striking background, as of another hill-crowned Athens, is most complete and satisfying. The colouring throughout, diversified with extreme art as it is, is full of that southern radiance, and clear, sunlit glamour, so often found in the artist's pictures. To realize this fully, South Kensington must be visited, for word-painting at its best but poorly reproduces the art that it doubtfully imitates.

But these were by no means the first attempts of the artist to acclimatize the noblest form of mural decoration, which cannot even at this date be regarded as fully naturalized amongst us. In 1866 he commenced work on a fresco of *The Wise and Foolish Virgins*, which forms the altarpiece of the beautiful modern church at Lyndhurst, erected on the site of the older building commemorated in Charles Kingsley's ballad. This painting still remains a lasting attraction to visitors in the New Forest village. In the centre, the Bridegroom, clad in white, bearing lilies in His left hand, extends His right to the foremost of the five wise virgins. Angels at each side of the central figure welcome the one group, and repel the other. On the extreme right is a kneeling figure, "Ora;" on the left, "Vigila," a figure trimming a lamp. The scale of the figures is over life-size, and the unfortunate position of the work, immediately under a large east window, so that the figures appear standing on the altar, has provoked adverse criticism; but the painting itself, as a triumphant accomplishment of a peculiarly difficult undertaking, and a superb scheme of line and colour, has won favourable comments at all times. It was painted in the medium, a mixture of copal, wax, resin, and oil, previously employed with success by Mr. Gambier Parry in his decorations for Ely Cathedral.

It is interesting to read the account of the execution of this work, which is said to have been carried out chiefly on Saturday afternoons, the artist catching a mid-day train from town, and working on it from the moment of his arrival until dusk. Experience of the London and South Western Railway Company thirty years ago makes one doubt whether leaving town at mid-day should not be taken as arriving at Lyndhurst Road at that time, for otherwise it would have been a miracle to accomplish the task by daylight. It is, however, exhilarating to find that the sustained enthusiasm of the young artist was equal to the effort involved in mastering so many obstacles; for the result, despite the increased attention given to decoration in these later years, may even now be considered, so far as modern ecclesiastical painting is concerned, to be without a rival in England.

The beautiful *Cupid with Doves*, is also said to be from a fresco; whether a genuine painting on the wall itself (after the true fresco manner) or not, it has the larger qualities peculiar to the method which distinguishes several other works that were certainly not executed in this medium, – the latest of Leighton's mural decorations, for example, a painting of *Phœnicians Bartering with Britons*, which the President of the Royal Academy in 1895 presented as the first of a series of panels in the Royal Exchange. Although, as this was painted on canvas, it cannot be ranked as a legitimate successor in the direct line of the Lyndhurst and South Kensington frescoes, it is marked by many of the architectural qualities which distinguish a painting designed to be in true relation to the planes of its surroundings, and employs a convention which makes it appear an integral part of the wall surface, not a mere panel accidentally placed within a frame supplied by the features of the building itself.

The South Kensington frescoes, as we have before stated, were painted in 1872-3. Some ten years later Sir Frederic collaborated with Sir Edward (then Mr.) Poynter in the decoration of the dome of St. Paul's. His share was to have filled eight *medallions*, so called, in the compartments into which his colleague divided the dome. The design for one of these, *The Sea gave up the Dead which were in it*, was exhibited at the Academy of 1892, and is now among the works presented by Mr. Tate to the National Gallery of British Art. This is another treatment of a great subject, in which the problem of reconciling the dramatic with the decorative has been seriously attempted. The dome of St. Paul's, had it been completed according to this scheme, might have been a worthy if a somewhat academic presentation of the tremendous visions of the Apocalypse.

Not so well known is his frieze delineating a dance, for an English drawing-room; or the small frieze with a design of Dolphins, also in England. A scheme in water-colours for a mural decoration, entitled *The Departure for the War*, was never carried out; the sketch for it was sold with the remaining works at Christie's, July, 1896. The single figures in mosaic of *Cimabue* and *Pisano*, at the South Kensington Museum, must not be forgotten.

To the public – or at least that portion which limits its art to the exhibitions of the Royal Academy – Leighton, as we have seen, made his *début* as a sculptor with the group, *An Athlete struggling with a Python* (known also as *An Athlete strangling a Python*), which in the bronze version is now among works purchased under the terms of the Chantrey bequest in the Tate Gallery. But long before that date he had successfully essayed plastic art; his first effort being for the medallion of a monument to Mrs. Browning in the Protestant cemetery at Florence. Two other monuments, to the memory of Major Sutherland Orr (his sister's husband), and Lady Charlotte Greville, must also be mentioned. We have already spoken of *The Athlete, The Sluggard*, and *Needless Alarms*. But it would be unfair to omit mention of many small works – small, that is to say, in scale, for they are distinguished by great breadth of handling – which were prepared as auxiliary studies for his paintings. Visitors to the studio in Holland Park Road, were always impressed by several of these models, which stood on a large chest in the bay of a great studio window. Especially noteworthy was a group of three singing maidens, who figure in *The Daphnephoria,* and another of the "choragus" for the same picture; for later works, the mounted Perseus, and Andromeda with the monster, both designed for the picture of that legend. Others belonging to a slightly earlier period included – the sleeping Iphigenia, a crouching figure of her attendant, and a nude figure of Cymon, all, of course, for *Cymon and Iphigenia.* These models were made to be clad in wet drapery of exquisitely fine texture, and were prepared only for ten minutes' drawing of the first idea of the figures; all serious study being made from the draped model, or the lay figure. Such help as they have rendered must all be referred to the period before the finished cartoon was ready to be traced on the canvas. Since Lord Leighton's decease most of these have been successfully cast in bronze, and are the property of the Royal Academy. In the studio were also the first sketches in clay for *The Sluggard,* and also for *The Athlete,* which was not originally intended to be carried further. Indeed, several people mistook it for a genuine antique, and admired it accordingly; Dalou, the great French sculptor, was especially so struck by it, that he advised its author to work out the idea in full size. The three years' labour devoted to the task, the failures by the way, and its ultimate triumphant success, both here and in Paris, are too well known to need recapitulation. A replica was commissioned for the Copenhagen Gallery, and probably no work of its accomplished author did more to win him the appreciation of French and German artists.

In this brief mention of Lord Leighton's achievements in sculpture, the medal commemorating the Jubilee of Queen Victoria, a study for which is reproduced at p. 130, must not be overlooked.

Although to those who have not followed closely the splendid period of English illustration which may be said to have reached its zenith at the time when Dalziel's "Bible Gallery" was published, it may be a surprise to find "Frederic Leighton" figuring as an illustrator, yet the nine compositions in that book are by no means his sole contribution to the art of black and white.

For each instalment of "Romola," as it ran through the pages of the "Cornhill Magazine," the artist contributed a full page drawing, and an initial letter. The twenty-four full pages were afterwards reprinted in "The Cornhill Gallery" (Smith and Elder, 1865). These are most notable works, even when measured by the standard of their contemporaries. The same magazine contains two other works from his pen, one illustrating a poem, "The great God Pan," by Mrs. Browning, and another illustrating a story by Mrs. Sartoris, entitled "A Week in a French Country House." These, and the nine compositions in the "Bible Gallery" (the pictures from which have lately been re-issued in a popular form by the Society for Promoting Christian Knowledge) exhaust the list of those which can be traced. As four of the magnificent designs are reproduced here, it would be superfluous to describe them; the titles of the five others are: *Abram and the Angel*, *Eliezer and Rebekah*, *Death of the First Born*, *The Spies' Escape*, and *Samson at the Mill*.

One of the original drawings on wood is now on view at the South Kensington Museum, and, by comparison with impressions from the engraved blocks, we see how small has been the loss in translation, so admirably has the artist mastered the limitation of the technique that was to represent his work in another medium. The reproductions here given are considerably reduced, and necessarily lose something, but they retain enough to prove that had the artist cared to rest his reputation upon such works, he might have done so with a light heart, for whenever the golden period of English illustration is recalled, these comparatively few drawings will inevitably be recalled with it.

A photographic silver-print from a drawing which forms the frontispiece to a little book of fairy tales is of hardly sufficient importance – charming though its original must have been – to be included among the book illustrations. The drawing, *A Contrast*, reproduced at p. 72, is undated; the idea it is intended to suggest, a model who once stood for some youthful god, revisiting the adolescent portrait of himself when old age has him gripped fast with rheumatism and failing vigour.

To-day, when one has heard sculptors claim that Lord Leighton's finest work was in their own craft, one has also heard many illustrators not merely extol these drawings – notably the Bible subjects – as his masterpieces, but jealously refuse to consider him entitled to serious regard as an artist in any other medium. This attitude, so curiously unlike the usual welcome from experts which awaits an artist who ventures into fresh mediums for expressing himself, should be put on record as a unique tribute; the more worthy of attention, because in each instance it was advanced not wholly as praise, but to some extent as a reproach on Leighton's painting. No intended compliment could carry more genuine appreciation than this warm approval from fellow experts in the special subjects of which they are masters.

CHAPTER VIII

Discourses on Art

We must next speak of the late President's Addresses and Discourses on Art, and of that other art of oratory, which, we shall find, as he conceived it, had something of the same monumental quality he imparted to his painting. His presidential speeches at the annual banquet of the Academy would alone be sufficient to show this; but it is of course to his Addresses and Discourses that we must turn if we would understand his feeling for the two unallied arts.

His success in the one is to be explained, we shall find, in very much the same way as his success in the other. Like most speakers of any distinction, Lord Leighton left nothing to chance. In his speeches and Discourses, as in his pictures, the most careful and exact preparation was made for every effect, however apparently casual it may have seemed. His Discourses were obviously based upon classic models; for their full periods, sonorously and deliberately arranged, have a rhythm that attends to the whole period, and not merely, as is often the way with English speakers, to each sentence in turn.

In quoting from these Discourses, we do so, however, with an eye to his own proper art as a painter, and to his whole theory and sentiment of that art and its functions, and its allied plastic arts, even more than to his art as a speaker. Indeed, the Discourses form a unique contribution to the art criticism of our time; they cover the most interesting and various periods in the history of the Art of Europe; and although the cycle he had mapped out was interrupted before he had completed it – first by illness which postponed the biennial discourse, and then by death – the portions already delivered touch incidentally on the theory and philosophy of all Art in a highly suggestive and eloquent way.

In his first Discourse, delivered to the Academy students on the 10th of December, 1879, the new President took occasion to estimate the modern predicament and general position of Art, as a prelude to the consideration of its special developments, in later Discourses. "I wish in so doing," he said, "to seek the solution of certain perplexities and doubts which will often, in these days of restless self-questioning in which we live, arise in the minds and weigh on the hearts of students who think as well as work."

In answering the question of questions in Art for us to-day – that is, what are its chances in the present, compared with the glory and splendour of its achievement in the past? – Leighton provides us with some memorable passages in his first Discourse. Speaking of the "Evolution of Painting in Italy," he turned it to notable account in his argument, as in this reference to the Florentine school:

"It is, perhaps," he said,

"in Tuscany, and notably in Florence, that we see the national temperament most clearly declared in its art, as indeed in all its intellectual productions; here we see that strange mixture of Attic subtlety and exquisiteness of taste, with a sombre fervour and a rude Pelasgic strength which marks the Tuscans, sending forth a Dante, a Brunelleschi, and a Michael Angelo, – a Fiesole, a Boccaccio, and a Botticelli, and we find that eagerness in the pursuit of the knowledge of men and things, which was so characteristic of them, summed up in a Macchiavelli and a Lionardi da Vinci."

How different the conditions when we turn to consider English Art, as it stands to-day:

> "The whole current of human life setting resolutely in a direction opposed to artistic production; no love of beauty, no sense of the outward dignity and comeliness of things, calling on the part of the public for expression at the artist's hands; and, as a corollary, no dignity, no comeliness for the most part, in their outward aspect; everywhere a narrow utilitarianism which does not include the gratification of the artistic sense amongst things useful; the works of artists sought for indeed, but too often as a profitable merchandise, or a vehicle of speculation, too often on grounds wholly foreign to their intrinsic worth as productions of a distinctive form of human genius, with laws and conditions of its own."

The modern student may well question, whether the great artists of the past, if they lived now under our different conditions, would achieve all that they did then. For further bewilderment, the differences to be seen in the past itself, between school and school, and one age and another, may lead him to doubt "whether Art be not indeed an ephemeral thing, a mere efflorescence of the human intelligence, an isolated development, incapable of organic growth." To such doubts, comes the reassuring answer: "That Art is fed by forces that lie in the depth of our nature, and which are as old as man himself; of which therefore we need not doubt the durability; and to the question whether Art with all its blossoms has but one root, the answer we shall see to be: Assuredly it has; for its outward modes of expression are many and various, but its underlying vital motives are the same."

The new President concluded his first Discourse with an eloquent plea for sincerity in Art: "Without sincerity of emotion no gift, however facile and specious, will avail you to win the lasting sympathies of men" – a truth which perhaps needs more repeating to-day than ever it did!

In the second Discourse (December 10th, 1881), we are called upon to consider that other question which has so often perplexed the artist, especially the English artist, in whom the moral sentiment is apt to take a threatening form on occasion: "What is the relation in which Art stands to Morals and to Religion?"

For his reply, Leighton took in turn the two contentions: one, that the first duty of all artistic productions is the inculcation of a moral lesson, if not indeed of a Christian truth; the other, that Art is altogether independent of ethics. His conclusion is the only sagacious and sane one: that whilst Art in itself is indeed independent of ethics, yet is there no error so deadly as to deny that "the moral complexion, the ethos, of the artist does in truth tinge every work of his hand, and fashion, in silence, but with the certainty of fate, the course and current of his whole career." The steps that lead irresistibly to this conclusion, are very clearly indicated in the course of this Discourse; and the more convincingly, because the speaker is himself so sympathetic to the religious inspiration of Italian art, on the one hand, and to its merely natural æsthetic growth on the other.

"The language of Art," he said then,

"is not the appointed vehicle of ethic truths;... On the other hand, there is a field in which she has no rival. We have within us the faculty for a range of emotion, of exquisite subtlety and of irresistible force, to which Art, and Art alone amongst human forms of expression, has a key; these then, and no others, are the chords which it is her appointed duty to strike; and form, colour, and the contrasts of light and shade are the agents through which it is given to her to set them in motion. Her duty is, therefore, to awaken those sensations directly emotional and indirectly intellectual, which can be communicated only through the sense of sight, to the delight of which she has primarily to minister. And the dignity of these sensations lies in this, that they are inseparably connected by association of ideas with a range of perception and feelings of infinite variety and scope. They come fraught with dim complex memories of all the evershifting spectacle of inanimate creation and of the more deeply stirring phenomena of life; of the storm and the lull, the splendour and the darkness of the outer world; of the storm and the lull, the splendour and the darkness of the changeful and the transitory lives of men."

In his third Discourse, which was delivered on the 10th December, 1883, the President entered on his exhaustive discussion, continued in many subsequent Discourses, of "The relation of Artistic Production to the conditions of time and place under which it is evolved, and to the characteristics of the races to which it is due." In this Discourse he briefly and suggestively reviews the Art of Egypt, Assyria, and Greece, endeavouring to account for the main characteristics of each. In Egypt he shows how a nation securely established in a peace and pre-eminence lasting for ages, blessed beyond measure in a fertile and prospering climate, a nation beyond all things pious and occupied in reverential care of the dead, should give birth to an art serene, magnificent, and vast. "Those whose fortune it has been," he eloquently said, "to stand by the base of the Great Pyramid of Khoofoo, and look up at its far summit flaming in the violet sky, or to gaze on the wreck of that solemn watcher of the rising sun, the giant Sphinx of Gizeh, erect, still, after sixty centuries in the desert's slowly rising tide; or who have rested in the shade of the huge shafts which tell of the pomp and splendour of hundred-gated Thebes; must, I think, have received impressions of majesty and of enduring strength which will not fade within their memory."

After old Egypt, and the account of Chaldæan and Assyrian Art, with its warlike expression, we are led on in turn to the consideration of Greek Art, and the causes of its development. "Nothing that I am aware of in the history of the human intelligence," he said, "is for a moment comparable to the dazzling swiftness of the ripening of Greek Art in the fifth century before Christ." After speaking of the fortunate balance and interaction of races which resulted in the Greek Art of that era, he goes on to speak of the exceptionally favouring circumstances of the people: "Here are no vast alluvial plains, such as those along which, in the East, whole empires surged to and fro in battle; no mighty flood of rivers, no towering mountain walls: instead, a tract of moderate size; a fretted promontory thrust out into the sea – far out, and flinging across the blue a multitude of purple isles and islets towards the Ionian, kindred, shores." Such a fortunate environment, joined to the extraordinarily high ideal formed by the Greeks of citizenship, had much to do with the fostering of Greek Art, in all "its nobility and its serenity, its exquisite balance, its searching after truth, and its thirst for the ideal."

In his fourth Discourse Lord Leighton carried on his inquiry upon the origins and conditions of Art into the difficult region of the Etruscans; whose plastic work, like their speech, he considers, was at best an uncouth, vigorous imitation, or re-shaping, of Greek models. As examples of Etruscan Art, we are referred to "the two lovely bronze mirrors, preserved at Perugia and Berlin, representing, – one, Helen between Castor and Pollux, – the other, Bacchus, Semele, and Apollo... In either case, the design is distinctly Greek; nevertheless a certain ruggedness of form and handling is felt in both, betraying a temper less subtle than the Hellenic; and we read without surprise on the one 'Pultuke,' and 'Phluphluus' on the other." Lest it should be thought that something less than justice is done to Etruscan Art, take this fine description of the tomb of Volumnus Violens:

> "The recumbent effigy of the Volumnian is, indeed, rude and of little merit; rude also in execution is the monument on which it rests, but in conception and design of a dignity almost Dantesque. Facing the visitor, as he enters the sepulchral chamber, this small sarcophagus – small in dimensions, but in impressiveness how great! – rivets him at once under the taper's fitful light. Raised on a rude basement, the body of the monument figures the entrance to a vault; in the centre, painted in colours that have nearly faded, appears a doorway, within the threshold of which four female figures gaze wistfully upon the outer world; on either side two winged genii, their brows girt with the never-failing Etruscan serpents, but wholly free from the quaintness of early Etruscan treatment, sit cross-legged, watching, torch in hand, the gate from which no living man returns. Roughly as they are hewn, it would be difficult to surpass the stateliness of their aspect or the art with which they are designed; Roman gravity, but quickened with Etruscan fire, invests them: ... and our thoughts are irresistibly carried forward to the supreme sculptor whom the

Tuscan land was one day to bear."

From Etruria, we pass naturally on to Rome; for, as we are significantly reminded, "The Romans lay, until the tide of Greek Art broke on them after the fall of Syracuse, wholly under the influence of the Etruscans… Etruria gave them kings, augurs, doctors, mimes, musicians, boxers, runners; the royal purple, the royal sceptre, the fasces, the curule chair, the Lydian flute, the straight trumpet, and the curved trumpet. The education of a Roman youth received its finishing touches in Etruria: Tuscan engineers had girt Rome with walls; Tuscan engineers had built the great conduit through which the swamp, which was one day to be the Forum, was drained into the Tiber. What wonder, then, that in architecture, also in painting, in sculpture, in jewellery, and in all the things of taste, Etruscans gave the law to the ruder and less cultured race?"

This influence lasted, until the counter-current of Greece found an inlet to Roman life, filtering "through Campania into Rome from the opposite end of the peninsula." And then, from the fall of Syracuse, and the bringing of its spoils to Rome, we find a perfect craze for Grecian marbles, bronzes, pictures, gems, inflaming the magnates, nobles, and *nouveaux riches* of Rome. How fortunate that influence was in another field, that of literature, we know. In plastic art, by reason of the essentially inartistic spirit of the Roman race, the result was practically small; save indeed in one department, that of portraiture, to which the essential impulse was, as Leighton very suggestively shows, "ethic, not æsthetic." Even in Roman architecture, our critic finds little to weaken his view of the Roman æsthetic inefficiency. "It was not," he said, "the spontaneous utterance of an æsthetic instinct, but the outcome of material needs and of patriotic pride," and hence only an incomplete expression of Roman civilization. "To them, in brief, art was not vernacular: their purest taste, their brightest gifts of mind, found no utterance in it."

"We have seen Art," he concluded,

"such Art as it was given to Rome to achieve – rise and fall with the virtues of the Roman people. From the lips of the most seeing of its sons we know the solvent in which those virtues perished: that solvent was the greed, the insatiate greed, of gold – 'auri sacra fames' – the rot of luxury. 'More deadly than arms,' Juvenal magnificently exclaims, 'luxury has swept down upon us, and avenges the conquered world.'

......   'Sævior armis
Luxuria incubuit, victumque ulciscitur orbem.'"

From Rome we are taken, in the fifth Discourse, delivered on the 10th December, 1887, to the making and the racial re-shaping of Italy, that began with the fifth century. All through these Discourses the speaker laid great stress upon the ethnological history of the European races, as he turned to one after another, and essayed to trace their artistic idiosyncracy and their artistic evolution. Italy is, to the ethnologist as well as to the art student, one of the most interesting countries in Europe. Rome almost alone, among the Italian provinces, retained her racial and æsthetic peculiarities, unaffected to the end of the chapter; and even when she wielded "the sceptre of the Christian world," still she produced no one flower of native genius, we are reminded, unless Giulio Romano, that "brawny and prolific plagiarist of Raphael," as Leighton well stigmatizes him, be thought a genius; which criticism forbid!

It was different with Tuscany, where the introduction of new racial elements had a distinct effect. This "new amalgam" produced in the field of Art, we are told, an infinitely nobler and more exquisite result than had grown out of the old conditions. Still, however, the old Etruscan allied grace and harsh strength lingered on in the art of Christian Etruria. "Of the subtle graces which breathe in that art, from Giotto to Lionardo, it is needless to speak; and surely in the rugged angularities of a Verocchio, a Signorelli, or a Donatello, and in the shadow of sadness which broods over so much of the finest Florentine work, the more sombre phase of the Etruscan temper still lives on."

In the end, if we try to account for the artistic power and mastery of one people in Italy, and the lack of that power in another, we are driven to the conclusion that the source of the artistic gift is hidden and obscure. One may cite the opposite examples of Venice and of Genoa, – the one so masterfully artistic; the other so impotent. And yet the same favouring conditions, *à priori*, might have seemed to exist for both.

With the intermingling of the peoples, and the rejuvenescence of the physical life, came the spiritual outburst of Christianity. And the influence, again, of Christianity upon Italian Art was immense. In place of joy in the ideals of bodily perfection, "loathing of the body and its beauty, as of the vehicle of all temptation, a yearning for a life in which the flesh should be shaken off, a spirit of awe, of pity, and of love, became the moving forces that shaped its creations."

After great religious periods, we often find that great scientific periods follow. The ethical impulse that religion gives, is converted into other forms of energy, by reason of man's awakened consciousness of the meaning of things, physical and material as well as spiritual.

In Italy a reaction against the Christian doctrine of the degradation of the flesh led to a new recognition of the beauty of man and of his physical environment. Anatomy and perspective were studied, accordingly, with a new sense of their significance in Art. The spirit of science led to "such amazing studies of leaf and flower as Lionardo loved to draw. Thus to Tuscan artists the new movement brought the love of nature, and the light of science."

We come upon Dante and Petrarch in this Discourse, in tracing the history of Italian Art during the centuries of transition: "With Dante we reach the threshold of the Renaissance. He stands on the verge of the middle ages; in him the old order ends. With Petrarch the new order begins." It is not so much as a poet, however, that Petrarch counts in this process from one period to another; but rather as an intellectual pioneer, leading the way into the great pagan world. Petrarch "was the first Humanist," in short.

We cannot stay to dwell upon the effect of the Humanists and all they stood for, good and evil, in Italian Art and Letters. We pass on, now, from Petrarch and the influence the movement had on Italian literature, to its effect on Italian Art. The Renaissance did not affect Art in the same way, as Botticelli may serve to show. "But perhaps," said the lecturer, "the various operations in the province of Art of the two main motive forces of the Renaissance – the impulse towards the scientific study of nature, and the impulse to reinstate the classic spirit – may be best illustrated by reference to Lionardo da Vinci, Raphael, and Michael Angelo." The passages in which Leighton characterised these three masters are among the most striking of all those uttered by him within the walls of the Academy. Lionardo's scientific "avidity of research," Raphael's "classic serenity," and Angelo's "mediæval ardour," are turned to admirable effect in the pages of this Discourse; and the tribute paid to them on the part of an English painter who has zealously sought to live and work in the light of their great examples, has indeed an interest that is personal, in a sense, as well as general and critical.

Take this concluding sentence upon Raphael:

"Whatever was best in the classic spirit was absorbed and eagerly assimilated by him, and imparted to the work of his best day that rhythm, that gentle gravity, and that noble plenitude of form, which are its stamp, and proclaim him the brother of Mozart and of Sophocles."

Or this, again, on Michael Angelo, as distinguishing him from Raphael:

"The type of human form which he lifted to the fullest expressional force is the last development of a purely indigenous conception of human beauty, whereas the type which we know as Raphaelesque is a classic ideal warmed with Christian feeling. Sublimely alone as

★ 100

Buonarotti's genius stands, towering and unapproached, … it does but mark the highest summit reached in the magnificent continuity of its evolution, by the purely native genius of Tuscan Art."

Having arrived at Tuscan Art, and at Michael Angelo, in whom it reaches its consummate development, we leave Italy, and turn now to the description of Art in Spain, given by Lord Leighton in his Discourse of December, 1889. And first we have some account of the extraordinarily various racial strains which were contributed to form the significant figure of the fifteenth-century Spaniard. On the ancient Iberian stock was grafted Celtic, Greek, Phœnician, and Carthaginian blood; and to these infusions succeeded the great invasion of the Visigoths of the fifth century.

"The Art of Spain," he said, "was, at the outset, wholly borrowed, and from various sources; we shall see heterogeneous, imported elements, assimilated sometimes in a greater or less degree, frequently flung together in illogical confusion, seldom, if ever, fused into a new, harmonious whole by that inner welding fire which is genius; and we shall see in the sixteenth century a foreign influence received and borne as a yoke" – (that of the Italian Renaissance) "because no living generative force was there to throw it off – with results too often dreary beyond measure; and, finally, we shall meet this strange freak of nature, a soil without artistic initiative bringing forth the greatest initiator – observe, I do not say the greatest artist – the greatest initiator perhaps since Lionardo in modern art – except it be his contemporary Rembrandt – Diego Velasquez."

In his Discourse of December, 1891, we have, rapidly sketched, the Evolution of Art in France. Touching again on the question of race, the lecturer adduced the great race of Gauls, submitting first to Roman, and afterwards to Frankish, or Teutonic, domination and admixture. The main characteristics of the Gaulish people he judges to be, "a love of fighting and a magnificent bravery, great impatience of control, a passion for new things, a swift, brilliant, logical intelligence, a gay and mocking spirit – for 'to laugh,' says Rabelais, 'is the proper mark of man,' – an inextinguishable self-confidence." With the reign of Charlemagne began the development of the architecture of France, but not until the tenth and eleventh centuries did the "movement reach its full force; and its development was due mainly to the great monastic community, which, founded by St. Benedict early in the sixth century, had poured from the heights of Monte Cassino its beneficent influence over Western Europe."

Here we have it explained how the principle of Gothic architecture, "the substitution of a balance of active forces for the principle of inert resistance," was gradually evolved. This principle once found, Gothic architecture reached its most splendid period in a wonderfully short space of time; cathedrals and churches were built everywhere, and before the end of the thirteenth century, the most splendid Gothic buildings were begun or completed. With the end of the thirteenth century Gothic architecture began to decline, lured by the "fascination of the statical *tour de force*, the craving to bring down to an irreducible minimum the amount of material that would suffice to the stability of a building extravagantly lofty."

Many more extracts we would gladly make, whether from the account of the French sculpture of this period, marked as it was by "sincerity and freshness, often by great beauty and stateliness;" or from the criticism of such artists as Jean Cousin, who painted windows which were "limpid with hues of amethyst, sapphire, and topaz, and fair as a May morning;" or again, of Watteau, of whom we are told that "in the vivacity and grace of his drawing, in the fascination of his harmonies, rich and suave at once, in the fidelity with which he reflected his times without hinting at their coarseness, this wizard of the brush remains one of the most interesting, as he is one of the most fascinating, masters of his country's art."

In the Discourse of 1893 the History of Gothic Architecture was pursued, from its native France to its adopted home in Germany. At the end of last century Goethe declared that not only was the

Gothic style native to Germany, but no other nation had a peculiar style of its own; "for," he said, "the Italians have none, and still less the Frenchmen"! According to Leighton, "the Germans, as a race, were, speaking broadly, never at one in spirit with ogival architecture. The result was such as you would expect; in the use of a form of architecture which was not of spontaneous growth in their midst, and unrestrained, moreover, as they were, by a sound innate instinct of special fitness, German builders were often led into solecisms, incongruities, and excesses, from which in the practice of their native style they have been largely free." Of this style, which may be called the German-Romanesque, the best examples are to be found among the churches of the Rhineland. In the thirteenth century this style, admirably as it expressed the genius of the Teuton, succumbed to invading French influence. "I have often wondered," he continued, "at the strange contrast between the reticent and grave sobriety of the architecture of Germany before the fall of the Hohenstaufens, and its erratic self-indulgence in the Gothic period." There is much, however, to be said in praise of the Gothic churches of Germany, their fine colouring, suggestiveness, and variety. Take the description of the Church of St. Lorenz in Nuremberg. "Nothing could well be more delightful than the impression which you receive on entering it; the beauty of the dark brown stone, the rich hues of the stained glass, the right relation of tone value, to use a painter's term, between the structure and the lights – the sombre blazoned shields which cluster along the walls, the succession on pier beyond pier of pictures powerful in colour and enhanced by the gleaming gold of fantastic carven frames, above all the succession of picturesque objects in mid-air above you, a large chandelier, a stately rood-cross, and to crown all, Veit Stoss's masterpiece, the Annunciation, rich with gold and colour; all these things conspire to produce a whole, delightful and poetic, in spite of much that invites criticism in the architectural forms themselves." Still more interesting is the word-picture of the great Cathedral of Cologne, "a monument of

★ 103

indomitable will, of science, and of stylistic orthodoxy ... its beautiful rhythm, its noble consistency and unity, its soaring height, rivet the beholder's gaze"; and yet, the building, in spite of all, does not entirely convince: "the kindling touch of genius" seems to be wanting.

Take, finally, this description of Albert Dürer: "He was a man of a strong and upright nature, bent on pure and high ideals, a man ever seeking, if I may use his own characteristic expression, to make known through his work the mysterious treasure that was laid up in his heart; he was a thinker, a theorist, and as you know, a writer; like many of the great artists of the Renaissance, he was steeped also in the love of science... Superbly inexhaustible as a designer, as a draughtsman he was powerful, thorough, and minute to a marvel, but never without a certain almost caligraphic mannerism of hand, wanting in spontaneous simplicity – never broadly serene. In his colour he was rich and vivid, not always unerring in his harmonies, not alluring in his execution – withal a giant."

With this tribute to a great predecessor we must leave these Discourses, which need, to be properly appreciated, to be studied as a whole; as indeed they form Leighton's deliberate exposition of his whole principles of Aesthetics. In working this out, Discourse by Discourse, he was not content to rely upon convenient literary sources, or previously acquired knowledge of his subject; but undertook special journeys, and spent long periods, abroad, to procure his own evidence at first hand. This gives his Discourses all the value of original research, based on new materials, to add to their purely critical value. Had they been completed, they would have formed an invaluable contribution to the history and the philosophy of Art.

CHAPTER IX

Lord Leighton's Home

If we seek for practical expression of Leighton's sympathy for decorative art, we may find it most satisfactorily in his own home as it appeared during his life. Mr. George Aitchison, R.A., designed the whole house; – even the Arab Hall being largely built from drawings made specially by him in Moorish Spain. Although the exterior of No. 2, Holland Park Road has individuality, rather than distinction, it was within that its special charms were found. One of the first things seen on entering was a striking bronze statue, "Icarus," by Mr. Alfred Gilbert; a typical instance of Leighton's generous recognition of artistic contemporaries.

In earlier pages we spoke of the Arab Hall and its Oriental enchantment. No attempt to paint the effects of such an interior in words can call it up half as clearly as the slightest actual drawing. There is a dim dome above, and a fountain falling into a great black marble basin below; there are eight little arched windows of stained glass in the dome; and there are white marble columns, whose bases are green, whose capitals are carved with rare and curious birds, supporting the arches of the alcoves. The Cairo lattice-work in the lower arched recesses lets in only so much of the hot light of midsummer (for it is in summer that one should see it to appreciate its last charm), as consists with the coolness, and the quiet, and the perfect Oriental repose, which give the chamber its spell.

More in what we may call the highway of the house, from entrance hall to studios, is the large hall, out of which the Arab Hall leads, and from which the dark oak staircase ascends with walls tiled in blue and white. Here, on every side, one saw all manner of lovely paintings and exquisite *bric-à-brac*: a drawing of *The Fontana della Tartarughe in Rome* by Leighton's old mentor, Steinle; other bronzes and paintings, and in full view a huge stuffed peacock, which seemed to have shed some of its brilliant hues upon its surroundings.

In the drawing-room hung many Corots and Constables, with a superb Daubigny, and a most tempting example of George Mason, – a picture of a girl driving calves on a windy hill, amid a perfect embarrassment of such artistic riches. The famous Corots, a sequence of panels, representing *Morning, Noon, Evening,* and *Night*, which cost Lord Leighton less than 1,000 francs each, were sold for 6,000 guineas for the four, at Christie's, in July, 1896. Still another small Corot, a picture of a boat afloat on a still lake, was also in this room. One of the Constables that hung there is literally historic – for it is the sketch for that famous *Hay Wain* which, exhibited in Paris, at once upset the classical tradition, and gave impetus to the whole modern school of French landscape. Near it was one of Constable's many pictures of Hampstead Heath, – simply a bit of dark heath against a sympathetic sky; but so painted as to be a masterpiece of its kind. These pictures were but a few of the many artfully disposed things of beauty, born in older Italy, or newer France, or in our new-old London.

Upon the staircase there were pictures at every turn to make one pause, step by step, on the way. Sir Joshua Reynolds was represented by an unfinished canvas of Lord Rockingham, in which the great Burke, in his minor function of secretary, also figures. Then came G. F. Watts's earlier portrait of Leighton himself; and here a genuine Tintoretto. There was the P.R.A.'s famous *Portrait of Captain Burton*; and over a doorway his early painting of *The Plague at Florence*, with another early work, *Romeo and Juliet*, one of his very few Shakespearean pictures.

From the landing whence most of these things were visible, you entered at once the great studio. Round the upper wall ran a cast of the Parthenon frieze, and beneath this the wall on one side was riddled and windowed, as it were, with innumerable framed pictures, small studies of foreign scenes; so that one looked out in turn upon Italy and the South, Egypt and the East, or upon an Irish sunset, or a Scottish mountain-side.

Opposite these, below the great window, were many of the artist's miniature wax models and studies. Else, the ordinary not unpicturesque lumber of an artist's studio was conspicuously absent. The secret of Leighton's despatch and careful ordering of his days, was to be read, indeed, in every detail of his work-a-day surroundings. Even in a dim antechamber, with a trellised niche most mysteriously overlooking the Arab Hall, at one end of the studio, in which the curious visitor might have expected to find dusty studies, discarded canvases, and other such æsthetic remnants, – even that was found to contain not lumber, but a Sebastian del Piombo, a sketch of Sappho by Delacroix, a landscape by Costa, a Madonna and Child of Sano di Pietro del Piombo.

At the extreme other end of the main studio was the working studio of glass, built to combat the fogs by procuring whatever vestige of light Kensington may accord in its most November moods. The last addition to the building, not long before Lord Leighton's death, was a gallery, known as "The Music Room," expressly designed to receive his pictures – mostly gifts from contemporary artists; or, to speak more accurately, works that had been exchanged for others in a wholly non-commercial spirit. These included, *Shelling Peas*, by Sir J. E. Millais, *The Corner of the Studio*, by Sir L. Alma-Tadema, *The Haystacks*, and *Venus*, by G. F. Watts, and *Chaucer's Dream of Good Women*, by Sir E. Burne-

Jones.

Such was the daily environment of that hard, unceasing, indefatigable labour which, natural faculty taken for granted, is always the secret of an artist's extraordinary production. And it was an environment, as one felt on leaving it for the gray London without, that well accorded with the radiant painted procession of the figures, classic and other, that file through Lord Leighton's pictures.

CHAPTER X

Lord Leighton's House in 1900

In the preceding chapter a picture is drawn of the "House Beautiful," as it was in Lord Leighton's lifetime. It was then full to overflowing with all manner of treasures; but now all that were removable have been dispersed. Only the shell, the house itself, remains. Yet denuded as it is, that is still well worth looking at. The architectural features to which Mr. Rhys, dazzled by other things, hardly did justice, are now all the more apparent.

One of the rarest of all accomplishments, at any rate in England, is a cultivated taste in architecture; but it so happened that amongst his many acquirements Lord Leighton possessed it in a remarkable degree. In fact he received, although a painter by profession, the gold medal of the Royal Institute of British Architects in virtue of the intimate knowledge of architecture he had displayed in some of his backgrounds – for instance, those of the frescoes at South Kensington. It is a great honour, and one by no means lightly bestowed. At any rate, when there was a question of building himself a house, though he might not have been able to build it himself, he was thoroughly qualified to choose an architect. His choice fell upon Professor Aitchison, now R.A., and he probably hit upon the only man of his generation able to put his feeling into bricks and mortar, viz., the feeling for a beauty sedate, delicate, and dignified.

We must remember the condition of things architectural in the sixties to do justice to the independence of employer and architect. It was a time when the Albert Memorial was possible, and when men tried to guide their steps by the light of "The Seven Lamps of Architecture." A sentimental fancy for Gothic based on irrational grounds was all but universal, and it needed courage to avow a preference for the classical. The compromise in favour of quaintness and capricious prettiness which began under the name of the "Queen Anne style," and has contributed so many picturesque and pleasing buildings to our modern London, had not yet budded. Nor would it ever at any time of his life have thoroughly responded to Leighton's taste. So long as he could detect a defect he was dissatisfied, and extreme nicety is not what the Dutch style pretends to. It depends upon a picturesque combination of forms of no great refinement in themselves, but which give a varied skyline and a pretty play of light and shade. It amuses at the first glance, and as it rarely demands a second, it is well suited to turbid atmospheres, which blur outlines, and a chilly climate in which people cannot loiter out of doors. Moreover, the old-world memories it evokes, although in a minor degree than was the case with the Gothic, contribute to its facile popularity. But the classical taste is a love for form and delicate beauty of line *as such*, quite irrespective of any associations which may accompany them, or lamps, be they seven or seventy times seven. And to build his house in this style was the natural thing for a sculptor and fastidious seeker after the ideal in form. He found the man he wanted in Professor Aitchison.

We must go over the outside and inside of the house, but rapidly; for to do more than just indicate the points worth attention would be waste of effort. To convey an idea of the feelings produced by architecture is perhaps possible, but it is perfectly vain to hope to picture it or reproduce in words the actual beauties of proportion or of colour. Those who wish to verify them must see for themselves and examine the building carefully.

The aspect of the house as seen from the street is, it must be admitted, hardly symmetrical; but it is evident also that the first design has been much altered and added to. At one end the Arab Hall, with its dome and "bearded" battlements, is an obvious afterthought, in great contrast with the serious simplicity of the rest. And at the other end the glass studio, which was added later still, is also clearly an excrescence. The centre part was the original house, and the studio was the chief feature of it, and very much as it is now. It is, of course, on the north side, and the street, the south side, is occupied by small rooms which, with their repeated small openings, offer no great scope for designing. Still, the whole has that look of dignity which always accompanies high finish; and the entrance, far from being commonplace, because it has nothing quaint or surprising about it, has a certain ample serenity which it is rare to find. The mouldings of stonework and woodwork, few and simple as they are, are not taken out of a pattern-book, as is usually the case, but are specially designed each for its own position. All the refinement of a building consists in its mouldings, and no one has designed mouldings better than Professor Aitchison. A vast improvement has been made in this respect in the last twenty years or so, and it is largely due to his influence. At any rate he was one of the first and he remains the best of modern designers of mouldings. There are some fine examples of his work in the house.

On the north the house looks into a fair-sized garden, skilfully planted, so that it looks much larger than it is. In the mind of the writer this aspect is intimately bound up with the recollection of delightful Sunday mornings in summer, when he sat chatting on random subjects with the President, who, in slippers, a so-called "land and water hat," and a smock frock, leant back in a garden-chair and talked as no one else could. The quiet, the sun overhead, the grass under our feet, the green trees around us, and the house visible between them, form an ineffaceable picture

★ 111

of æsthetic contentment it is a delight to recall. It recurred every Sunday whenever the weather was fine and warm. Then it was that there was leisure to appreciate the admirable symmetry of the architecture; for in England it is so rare to sit out of doors where one may look at architecture that even if architects were to design exteriors with all the subtlety of a Brunelleschi or a Bramante, they would seldom get anyone to notice their work.

The studio occupies the whole of the upper story, and the architect had a good opportunity, as there was no need to cut it up as is the case when several rooms have to be provided for, by numerous uniform lights. Here, in the centre, is one great light between wide spaces of wall judiciously divided by string courses, and in the upper part on either side of the great window is a row of three small windows. At the east end is a small door leading into a pretty little Venetian balcony with stone parapet. The whole makes a very beautiful building, and the details and proportions are all worth examining.

This central part was what one saw through the trees as one sat in the garden. Less visible were the glass studio on its iron columns, an excellent piece of work, considering its few possibilities, and the Arab Hall at the other end. Of course the latter looks a little incongruous. It is a professed reproduction of Arab architecture, but carried out, like the rest of the house, with unstinted expense, care, and finish.

We will now go inside by the front door. The cornice of the ceiling of the vestibule first entered is singularly fine. Like every other good artist Professor Aitchison improved as he went on, and this is one of his latest designs in mouldings. When the entrance was altered some years before the President's death, an opportunity occurred for putting in a new ceiling.

Passing on into the hall one comes upon a very picturesque arrangement of staircase. It is lit from above by a broad skylight. The stairs begin to rise against the wall of the dining-room which is recessed; while on the first floor the wall of the studio is projected and carried on columns, beyond which the stairs rise. So that figures coming through the hall in the light, begin mounting the stairs in the shadow, and re-emerge into the light, as the stairs turn, with a very varied and striking effect. By the first short flight of steps, and between the two columns, is a seat made of a Persian chest or cassone, beautiful and unusual in shape, and richly inlaid. Lord Leighton bought it in Rhodes or Lindos, and was very proud of it. It could not be removed and sold with the rest of the treasures at Christie's as it was a "fixture." The floor of the hall is of marble mosaic, mostly black and white. Only one small piece by the dining-room door, a very agreeable design, is in pinkish marbles.

On the left, down a short passage, is the Arab Hall. It is so unlike anything else in Europe that its reputation has withdrawn all attention from the rest of the house. It certainly is a most sumptuous piece of work. Elsewhere Leighton satisfied his love of chastened form; in this room and its approach he gave full scope to his delight in rich colours. The general scheme is a peacock blue, known technically as Egyptian green, and gold, with plentiful black and white. Here and there tiny spots of red occur, but they are rare. The harmony begins in the staircase hall. The walls, except in the recessed part, where there are genuine oriental tiles, are lined to the level of the first floor with tiles of a fine blue, from the kilns of Mr. De Morgan, and the soffitt of the stairs is coloured buff, with gold spots. In the passage the tone increases in richness. The ceiling is silver and the cornice gold, while the walls, except for a fine panel of oriental tiles over the drawing-room door, are lined with the same tiles as the staircase. Then between two grand columns of red Caserta marble, with gilt capitals modelled by Randolph Caldecott, we pass into the Arab Hall itself, and we come upon the full magnificence of the effect. It is made up of polished marbles of many colours, gilt and sculptured capitals, alabaster, shining tiles, glistening mosaic of gold and colours, brass and copper in the hanging corona, and coloured glass in the little pierced windows, in fact, of every form of enrichment yet devised by Eastern or Western Art. From the floor, which is black and white, the tone rises through blue to lose itself in the gloom of a golden dome, sparsely lit by jewel-like coloured lights.

In the centre a jet of water springs up, to fall back into a basin of black marble. The form of the basin which deepens towards the centre in successive steps, is an adaptation of the pattern of a well-known oriental fountain. All is equally black in this pool, and the border unfortunately is barely distinguishable from the water. After a dinner party at which Sir E. Burne-Jones, Mr. Whistler, Mr. Albert Moore, and many others were present, I recollect how, when we were smoking and drinking coffee in this hall, somebody, excitedly discoursing, stepped unaware right into the fountain. Two large Japanese gold tench, whose somnolent existence was now for the first time made interesting, dashed about looking for an exit, and there was a general noise of splashing and laughter. The dark, apparently fathomless pool was rather a mistake. Mishaps like that just mentioned occurred, I believe, more than once. There had been at first a white marble basin, but it did not give satisfaction, because, being in several pieces, it leaked, whereas the black one is all cut out of one block, at great expense, of course. But the white had the advantage of lightness where light is none too plentiful. In our winter, when days are dark and cold, black pools, with marble columns and floors, tiled walls, and dim domes about them do not fall in with English notions of cosy woollen comfort. The season to do justice to this hall is when summer comes round. When the sun breaks through the lattice work of the musharabiyehs, and the light is thrown up on the storied tiles, and up the polished columns to the glinting mosaic, to die away in the golden cupola, the effect is indeed superb, and to sit on the divan, by the splash of the fountain, and look from the glories within to the green trees without, is to live not in London but in the veritable Arabian nights.

The hall is square. On one side is the entrance. In the centre of each of the other sides is a lofty arched recess. Those to the north and south are windows, shuttered with genuine musharabiyehs bought in Cairo and having deep cushioned divans. The recess to the west has only a small pierced window high up. It has a raised step, and in it used to stand certain bronze reproductions from Pompeii, with pots, vases, etc., now gone. Some of the tiles were bought in Damascus in 1873. The price paid was £200 for the complete tile surface of one room. What would they be worth now? Others, particularly the great inscription spoken of below, were bought later in Cairo, and the rest at odd times. Here and there are single tiles, but most of them are in sets forming fine panels. An interesting one, in the south-east corner, represents hawks clutching their prey, cheetahs and deer, a hunter, etc., and another has herons, fish, tortoises, deer, etc. Set into the woodwork in the western recess are four tiles with female figures. These are either Persian or come from the neighbourhood of Persia, for the Anatolian or Egyptian Mahommedan tolerated no representations of life. The rest repeat in pleasing variety the usual motives of oriental design, viz., vines, cypresses, pinks and vases, doorways (? the entrances of mosques), with hanging lamps, and conventional floral designs. Above the entrance runs the chief treasure, the grand series of tiles bearing the great inscription. It is about sixteen feet long. According to Mr. Harding Smith it may be translated thus:

"In the name of the merciful and long-suffering God. The Merciful hath taught the Koran. He hath created man and taught him speech. He hath set the sun and moon in a certain course. Both the trees and the grass are in subjection to him."

It cannot be said that there is anything very new in that. There rarely is in such inscriptions. There are three others, but so far as they have been deciphered they appear to be incomplete, and in two cases, at any rate, to much the same effect as the big one. Just pious reminders. The real interest of them lies in the decorative effect of the imposing procession of letters across the wall, and the splendour of their colours. For beauty and condition

★ 115

this great inscription is said to be without a rival in any collection in Europe.

Let into the woodwork panelling in the west bay there are two small lustred Persian tiles of the thirteenth century. They have been mutilated as to the faces of the figures by true believers. The rest belong to the sixteenth or early seventeenth centuries, a time when artistic production was stimulated by the commercial wealth brought by the trade of Venice and Genoa with the East through Anatolia, Damascus and Cairo.

Round three sides above the tiles runs a decorative mosaic frieze, by Walter Crane, of an arabesque design on a gold ground. It is a beautiful and fanciful piece of work in itself, and it serves moreover to blend the prevailing colour of the tiles with the gilding of the upper regions. But it does not continue round the fourth side, because over the entrance, above the great inscription, an oriel window of musharabiyeh work looks down into the hall from the first floor of the house.

The pierced windows, or at least eight of them, were brought from Cairo, and when bought had the original glass in them; but in the east the glass is stuck in with white of egg, and as they were, as usual, ill-packed, the glass all came out and was ground to fragments in the jolting of the journey. Only enough could be saved to fill the window in the upper part of the west recess opposite the entrance. The remainder had to be filled with English imitations.

Returning now to the staircase, we find it ends on the first floor in a landing leading to the great studio. On the left it is open to the little studio; so-called because, having a skylight, Lord Leighton used it for painting out-of-door effects until he had the glass studio built. Adjoining it, or forming an extension of it, is another room, built only a year or two before the late owner's death. After the addition of the glass studio the two were only used as an antechamber, and were hung with the pictures presented by brother artists, and with a few old masters. The mouldings round the skylights are very pretty. The latticed window before mentioned looks down from the little studio into the Arab Hall.

The great studio is a large room about sixty feet by twenty-five and about seventeen in height. In the centre of the north side is the lofty window forming a bay and extending into a skylight in the top. High up on either side of it are the three small openings mentioned when speaking of the exterior. A curtain hangs in front of them, and in point of fact they were never used. In the west wall is an apse with a gilt semi-dome, which appears in some of Lord Leighton's pictures. Across the east end runs a gallery at about eight feet from the floor with bookshelves under it on either side, and in the middle a broad passage leads into the glass studio, and still outside this is a wide balcony looking into the garden. Casts of a portion of the Panathenaic frieze of the Parthenon run along the upper part of the wall of the great studio, fit emblem of the lifelong devotion of the President to classic art. Such then is the workshop. Even now, comparatively bare as it is at the present moment of writing, this is one of the most picturesque suites of rooms in existence; but to see it on one of the grand occasions of Leighton's musical receptions was a very different sight and one not easily to be forgotten. Then when walls and easels were covered with pictures, when rare carpets hung from the gallery, flowers and palms filled the bay window, beautiful women and men of every form of distinction crowded the floor to listen to Joachim and Piatti, nothing was wanting which could give beauty or interest to the spectacle.

It will be seen that the house is still rich in artistic beauty and still has objects of value. But the most precious of its contents are after all its associations. Its floors have been trodden by all that was most notable in the society of its owner's day, people whose names alone would be an epitome of our times. It was also the workshop of a great artist. But, above all, it was the centre of a great influence which profoundly modified English art.

Whatever judgment the future may pass upon his own productions, the fact must never be lost sight of that even without them Leighton was a great man. Intellectually, spiritually, and socially he was the most brilliant leader and stimulator of artists we have ever seen in England. His earnest example and lifelong persistence fanned the flame of enthusiasm among all branches of art workers. He taught Englishmen to study form, and it was under his encouragement that sculpture, which was fallen so low, has now risen into so good a place. Finally he did more than anyone else has done to raise the status of the artist in society.

The house which he built himself was his hobby, and in the refinement and catholicity of taste it shows, there is so just a reflex of his characteristics that an account of it is indispensable to any book which claims to describe the man.

S. Pepys Cockerell.

CHAPTER XI

The Artist and his Critics

Before closing our record it will be well to quote, as we promised earlier, some of the contemporary criticism that Sir Frederic's work has encountered from time to time; and especially the criticism of his earlier performances, while he was still in the years of his pre-Academic probation.

As a provocation to criticism, most interesting of all is his picture, the *Cimabue's Madonna carried in Procession through the Streets of Florence*, upon which we have already commented. As we may here remind our readers, it was painted at Rome chiefly, in 1853-4, and was exhibited at the Academy of 1855. In that year, as good fortune would have it, Mr. Ruskin issued for the first time, "Notes on some of the Principal Pictures Exhibited in the Rooms of the Royal Academy." Some pages of this famous pronouncement are devoted to this very picture, and we cannot do better than quote freely from a criticism so remarkable.

"This is a very important and very beautiful picture," says Mr. Ruskin.

"It has both sincerity and grace, and is painted on the purest principles of Venetian art – that is to say, on the calm acceptance of the whole of nature, small and great, as, in its place, deserving of

★ 119

faithful rendering. The great secret of the Venetians was their simplicity. They were great colourists, not because they had peculiar secrets about oil and colour, but because when they saw a thing red, they painted it red; and … when they saw it distinctly, they painted it distinctly. In all Paul Veronese's pictures, the lace borders of the table cloths or fringes of the dresses are painted with just as much care as the faces of the principal figures; and the reader may rest assured that in all great art it is so. Everything in it is done as well as it *can* be done. Thus in the picture before us, in the background is the Church of San Miniato, strictly accurate in every detail; on the top of the wall are oleanders and pinks, as carefully painted as the church; the architecture of the shrine on the wall is well studied from thirteenth-century Gothic, and painted with as much care as the pinks; the dresses of the figures, very beautifully designed, are painted with as much care as the faces: that is to say, all things throughout with as much care as the painter could bestow. It necessarily follows that what is most difficult (*i.e.* the faces) should be comparatively the worst done. But if they are done as well as the painter could do them, it is all we have to ask; and modern artists are under a wonderful mistake in thinking that when they have painted faces ill, they make their pictures more valuable by painting the dresses worse.

"The painting before us has been objected to because it seems broken up in bits. Precisely the same objection would hold, and in very nearly the same degree, against the best works of the Venetians. All faithful colourists' work, in figure-painting, has a look of sharp separation between part and part… Although, however, in common with all other works of its class, it is marked by these sharp divisions, there is no confusion in its arrangement. The principal figure is nobly principal, not by extraordinary light, but by its own pure whiteness; and both the Master and the young Giotto attract full regard by distinction of form and face. The features of the boy are carefully studied, and are indeed what, from the existing portraits of him, we know those of Giotto must have been in his youth. The head of the young girl who wears the garland of blue flowers is also very sweetly conceived.

"Such are the chief merits of the picture. Its defect is that the equal care given to the whole of it is not yet *care enough*. I am aware of no instance of a young painter, who was to be really great, who did not in his youth paint with intense effort and delicacy of finish. The handling here is much too broad; and the faces are, in many instances, out of drawing, and very opaque and feeble in colour. Nor have they in general the dignity of the countenance of the thirteenth century. The Dante especially is ill-conceived – far too haughty, and in no wise noble or thoughtful. It seems to me probable that Mr. Leighton has greatness in him, but there is no absolute proof of it in this picture; and if he does not, in succeeding years, paint far better, he will soon lose the power of painting so well."

To Mr. Ruskin's account, which is sufficient to enable one to realize the picture in some detail, we may add further the criticism of the "Athenæum" of May 12th, 1855, which is interesting as showing how the work affected a contemporary critic of another order. It speaks of Mr. Leighton as "a young artist who, we believe, has studied in Italy," and goes on to say: "There can be no question that the picture is one of great power, although the composition is quaint even to sectarianism; and though the touch, in parts broad and masterly, is in the lesser parts of the roughest character." The last clause of the sentence bears out, it may be perceived, a significant indictment in Mr. Ruskin's deliverance, which lays stress on a defect that the artist, in his maturer brush-work, does not show.

Rossetti, writing to his friend William Allingham, May 11th, 1855, says:

"There is a big picture of *Cimabue*, one of his works in procession, by a new man, living abroad, named Leighton – a huge thing, which the Queen has bought, which everyone talks of. The R.A.'s have been gasping for years for someone to back against Hunt and Millais, and here they have him, a fact that makes some people do the picture injustice in return. It was *very* uninteresting to me at first sight; but on looking more at it, I think there is great richness of arrangement, a quality which, when *really* existing, as it does in the best old masters, and perhaps hitherto in no living man – at any rate English – ranks among the great qualities.

"But I am not quite sure yet either of this or of the faculty for colour, which I suspect exists very strongly, but is certainly at present under a thick veil of paint, owing, I fancy, to too much continental study. One undoubted excellence it has – facility, without much neatness or ultra-cleverness in the execution, which is greatly like that of Paul Veronese; and the colour may mature in future works to the same resemblance, I fancy. There is much feeling for beauty, too, in the women. As for purely intellectual qualities, expression, intention, etc., there is little as yet of them; but I think that in art richness of arrangement is so nearly allied to these, that where it exists (in an earnest man) they will probably supervene. However, the choice of subject, though interesting in a certain way, leaves one quite in the dark as to what faculty the man may have for representing incident or passionate emotion. But I believe, as far as this showing goes, that he possesses qualities which the mass of our artists aim at chiefly, and only seem to possess. Whether he have those of which neither they nor he give sign, I cannot tell; but he is said to be only twenty-four years old. There is something very French in his work, at present, which is the most disagreeable thing about it; but this I dare say would leave him if he came to England." [12]

In the year following Leighton's academical *début*, he exhibited a picture entitled *The Triumph of Music*, which the "Athenæum," hereafter so sympathetic towards his work, described as "anything but a triumph of art."

Partly, perhaps, because of the general tone of discouragement in all the criticisms of this year, the artist did not send in anything to the Academy of 1857. In 1858 his two pictures – *The Fisherman and the Syren*, and *Count Paris*, although admirably conceived, and extremely interesting to us now, received no word of friendly criticism that is worth recording.

At the Academy of 1859 were exhibited two pictures by him, which served to reassure at last those critics who had been shaking their heads over his supposed inability to follow up his first success. We turn to the "Athenæum" again, to study its gradual conversion from an attitude of critical distrust to one of critical sympathy:

"Mr. Leighton," says the "Athenæum," "after a temporary eclipse, struggles again to light. His heads of Italian women this year are worthy of a young old master: anything more feeling, commanding, or coldly beautiful, we have not seen for many a day... This is real painting, and we cannot but think that a painter who can paint so powerfully will soon be able to surpass that processional picture of his,..." *i.e.*, the *Cimabue*.

In 1860, the artist, who then entered upon his thirtieth year, exhibited a small picture, *Capri, Sunrise*, which won great praise for its successful treatment of Italian landscape under the Scirocco, whose sulphurous light is cast with evil suggestion upon the white houses and green vegetation. In paying his tribute to the quality of the picture, the critic of the "Athenæum" cannot resist, however, the old cry of great expectations. For the effect of the *Cimabue's Madonna* had aroused critics to regard the painter as one who would continue the legend of the great historical schools, and carry on the traditions of the so-called grand style. But the critic proposes, the creator disposes: the artist went his own way, following still his own ideals.

In 1861, some rather warm discussion raged over two of the artist's contributions to the Royal Academy, which appeared in its catalogue as Nos. 399 and 550, and which, it was said, had been deliberately slighted by the hanging committee. In later years, Leighton must sometimes have smiled when he heard (as from his position he must needs have,) the annual plaint of the "skied." It is to the "Art Journal," whose criticisms, when they had to do with the new and rising schools, used to be always entertaining, if often provoking, in those days, that we turn for a contemporary account of these things, rather than to any other source. The critic having premised, with a delightful and convincing air of "I told you so!" that his first effort (the inevitable *Cimabue's Madonna*) having exhausted the poor artist, "he has been coming down the ladder of fame ever since," continues in characteristic tones: "Instead of being hung too high, the *Dream*, had it been properly hung, would have been displayed upon the ceiling." The picture, according to this authority, consisted only of a questionable combination of the "lower forms of mere decorative ornamentation," and was in fact, "not so much a picture as a very clever treatment for the centre of a ceiling." So much for what was really the first clear sign of the artist's delightful decorative faculty.

It is clear from various evidences of the feeling of the critics about Leighton at this time, that they had begun to look upon him as one whose ideals were frivolous, and not seriously minded, or weighted with the true British substantiality of the old

Academy tradition. In the very next year, the artist, by the chances of his own temperamental many-sided delight in life and art, did something to reassure his admonitors once more. No. 217 at the Royal Academy of 1862 was his picture, *The Star of Bethlehem*, which, with some natural and not unfair deductions, won considerable praise from the critic last quoted. In this painting, which shows curiously the mingled academic and natural quality of the artist, the critic found profound incompatibilities of conception and technique; and next year, the same critic was stirred to exclaim, – "The pictures which of all others give most trouble and anxiety to the critic are perhaps those of Mr. Millais and Mr. Leighton," – a very suggestive conjunction of names, let us add.

It was probably the same critic, who speaking of the *Dante at Verona*, in 1864, said gravely, "The promise given by the *Cimabue* here reaches fruition."

Writing in 1863, Mr. W. M. Rossetti, a critic whom it is interesting to be able to cite, said of two of the artist's pictures of that year, the *Girl feeding Peacocks* and the *Girl with a Basket of Fruit*, they belong "to that class of art in which Mr. Leighton shines – the art of luxurious exquisiteness; beauty, for beauty's sake; colour, light, form, choice details, for their own sake, or for beauty's."

In the same year, Mr. Rossetti spoke of the young artist as the one "British painter of special faculty who has come forward with the most decided novelty of aim" – since, that is, the new development of art under the little band of Pre-Raphaelites, – with which Mr. W. M. Rossetti was himself so closely associated.

By way of contrast, we may cite the "Art Journal" of 1865, which provides a most extraordinary criticism of *David*, of that year. "We would venture to ask," says this ingenious critic, "why the divine psalmist has so small a brain? Within this skull there is not compass for the poet's thoughts to range. We state as a physiological fact, that a head so small, with a brow so receding, could not have belonged to any man who has made himself conspicuous in the world's history. Again, descending to mere matter of costume, there cannot be a doubt that the purple mantle flung on the psalmist's shoulders is wholly wanting in study of detail, and constitutes a blot on the landscape. Barring these oversights, the picture possesses merits."

At this period we hear the first critical murmurs against the artist's very deliberately chosen method of flesh-painting. In 1867, speaking of the *Venus Disrobing*, the "Art Journal" critic says: "According to the manner, not to say the mannerism, of the artist, it has a pale silvery hue, not as white as marble, not so life-glowing as flesh." With this we may compare, for the comparison is instructive, the "Athenæum," whose notice is more sympathetic. The figure of the goddess it describes as "all rosy white, ... admirably drawn, and modelled with extreme care."

Again, in 1868, the "Art Journal" says of Sir Frederic's *Actæa*: "The artist has made some attempt to paint flesh in its freshness and transparency, and indeed the more he renounces the opacity of the German school, and the more he can realize the brilliance of the old Venetian painters, the better."

In 1869, the "Athenæum" praised the *Sister's Kiss*, as "a lovely group," but complained that the execution was a "little too smooth," – a complaint not infrequently echoed from time to time by the artist's critics. Some years later we find Mr. W. M. Rossetti making the same complaint in criticising *Winding the Skein*.

In 1875 the picture, *Portions of the Interior of the Grand Mosque at Damascus*, won great praise, as "a remarkably delicate piece of work, in which the beautiful colouring of the tiled walls and mosaic pavement are skilfully rendered."

In 1876, the quondam hostile "Art Journal" is completely converted by the *Daphnephoria*: "To project such a scene upon canvas presupposes a man of high poetic imagination, and when it is accompanied by such delicacy and yet such precision of drawing and such sincerity of modelling, the poet is merged in the painter and we speak of such a one as a master. There is, indeed, nothing more consolatory to those who take an interest in

British art than the knowledge that we have among us a man of such pure devotion and lofty aim."

It was in 1875, that Mr. Ruskin, resuming his *rôle* of an Academy critic, claimed Leighton as "a kindred Goth," and confessed, "I determined on writing this number of 'Academy Notes,' simply because I was so much delighted with Mr. Leslie's *School*, Mr. Leighton's *Little Fatima*, Mr. Hook's *Hearts of Oak*, and Mr. Couldery's *Kittens*."

In his lectures on the Art of England, the same critic, speaking of Leighton's children, says: "It is with extreme gratitude, and unqualified admiration, that I find Sir Frederic condescending from the majesties of Olympus to the worship of those unappalling powers, which, heaven be thanked, are as brightly Anglo-Saxon as Hellenic; and painting for us, with a soft charm peculiarly his own, the witchcraft and the wonderfulness of childhood."

Upon the *Egyptian Slinger* of the same year, which Mr. Ruskin terms the "study of man in his Oriental function of scarecrow (symmetrically antithetic to his British one of game preserver)," his criticism is interesting, but adverse. The critic who elsewhere acknowledged fully the artist's acutely observant and enthusiastic study of the organism of the human body, confesses himself unable to recognize his skill, or to feel sympathy with the subjects that admit of its display. It is, he goes on to say further of the *Slinger*, "it is, I do not doubt, anatomically correct, and with the addition of the corn, the poppies, and the moon, becomes semi-artistic; so that I feel much compunction in depressing it into the Natural History class; and the more, because it partly forfeits its claim even to such position, by obscuring in twilight and disturbing our minds, in the process of scientific investigation, by sensational effects of afterglow and lunar effulgence, which are disadvantageous, not to the scientific observer only, but to less learned spectators; for when simple persons like myself, greatly susceptible to the influence of the stage lamps and pink side-lights, first catch sight of this striding figure from the other side of the room, and take it, perhaps, for the angel with his right foot on the sea and the left on the earth, swearing there shall be Time no longer; or for Achilles alighting from one of his lance-cast-long leaps on the shore of Scamander, and find on near approach that all this grand straddling and turning down of the gas mean practically only a lad shying stones at sparrows, we are only too likely to pass it petulantly without taking note of what is really interesting in this eastern custom and skill."

The most recent criticism of importance on the art of Leighton is contained in an admirable volume by M. de la Sizeranne. [13] We take this opportunity of quoting a few sentences from an appreciation which opens with the significant remark that Sir Frederic Leighton is officially the representative of English painting on the Continent, and, in reality, the representative of Continental painting in England, and concludes by tracing the definitely English ideal that underlies the artist's work. Elsewhere the critic says, "Ce qui est britannique en M. Leighton, quoique bien voilé par son éclectisme, transparaîtra encore." Apart from Leighton's distinctively native predilection for certain subjects, M. de la Sizeranne finds him very English in his treatment of draperies, for instance, a treatment which he traces ingeniously to the much study given to the Greek drapery of the Elgin marbles by the English School, since the days of the Pre-Raphaelites. Elsewhere, taking as his text the picture *The Spirit of the Summit*, he says: "Des sujets qui élèvent la pensée vers les sommets de la vie ou de l'histoire, de sorte qu'on ne puisse se rappeler un nez ou une jambe sans se souvenir de quelque haute leçon évangélique, ou de moins de quelque grande nécessité sociale, voilà ce que M. Leighton a traité. Et un style beaucoup plus sobre que celui d'Overbeck, beaucoup plus viril que celui de M. Bouguereau, voilà comment il les a traités." Again: "La grandeur de la communion humaine, la noblesse de la paix, tel est le thème qui a le plus souvent et le mieux inspiré M. Leighton. Et cela il ne l'a pas trouvé en France, ni ailleurs. C'est bien une idée anglaise." No better summing up of the chronicle of the life work

★ 127

of the artist could well be found.

But we have pursued far enough this study of an artist's progress through the thorny, devious ways of art criticism. We have reached the point, in fact, where the comparative uncertainties of an artist's career make way for the certainties. With one quotation more, in which we have a tribute from another critic, Mr. Comyns Carr, we may fitly close: "No painter of our time," said Mr. Carr, "maintains a firmer or more constant adherence to those severe principles of design which have received the sanction of great example in the past. Sir Frederic Leighton has never lowered the standard of his work in deference to any popular demand, and for this persistent devotion to his own highest ideals he deserves well of all who share his faith in the power of beauty."

CHAPTER XII

Conclusion

In now bringing this record to a close, we will of set purpose remain true to the chronicler's function, pure and simple; attempting no profounder or more critical summing up of our subject, than consists with the plain record of a remarkable career.

After a year of indifferent health, during part of which time he was ordered abroad for rest and change, being thus unable to preside at the annual banquet in May, Leighton returned to England apparently convalescent. Although unable to deliver the biennial presidential address, which fell due in December, 1895, he met the students on that occasion, and apologized for not delivering the Discourse which was due, in these words: "The cloud which has hung over me hangs over me still." [14]

Early in 1896 a peerage was bestowed upon him, and all the world applauded the honour conferred on Art in his name. On January 13th, 1896, the news of his death came as a terrible surprise. The new peer, Baron Leighton of Stretton, was buried with much state at St. Paul's Cathedral, before men in general had wholly recognized that Lord Leighton was the popular "Sir Frederic," the President of the Royal Academy, and one of the most familiar figures at any important function – at court or elsewhere.

Except perhaps in the case of politicians, who live in some degree by the public recognition of their personal qualities, it is difficult to render tribute gracefully and well to a contemporary. But we cannot close these pages, now, without pausing to recall how fortunate it has been that English Art, for seventeen years, had as its titular head an artist whose affluent artistic faculty was but the open sign of a crowded life, loyal throughout to the great causes, high ideals, and, let us add, the early friendships, chosen long ago in the mid century. We are now at that century's end, – an end not without its reproach, as expressed by a decadence more self-conscious than dignified, more critical than creative; but in Lord Leighton's Art there was little diminution in his active energy, and of that finer health and spirit of life, which is behind all beauty! Like his distinguished friend and colleague, Mr. G. F. Watts (whose tribute to him as a man and as an artist has been expressed again and again in eloquent terms), Leighton remained, in his later period as in his youth, generously alive to all the things that count, devoted still to the Art, the current life, and the great national traditions, of his own country.

From another famous colleague, Sir E. J. Poynter, P.R.A., one may fitly add here the following further sentences of contemporary tribute, which were written by way of dedication to his "Ten Lectures on Art," published some years ago:–

"I came to-day from the 'Varnishing Day' at the Royal Academy Exhibition with a pleasant conviction that there is on all sides a more decided tendency towards a higher standard in Art, both as regards treatment of subject and execution, than I have before noticed; and I have no hesitation in attributing this sudden improvement in the main to the stimulus given to us all by the election of our new President, and to the influence of the energy, thoroughness and nobility of aim which he displays in everything he undertakes. I was probably the first, when we were both young and in Rome together, to whom he had the opportunity of showing the disinterested kindness which he has invariably extended to beginners, and to him, as the friend and master who first directed my ambition, and whose precepts I never fail to recall when at work (as many another will recall them), I venture to dedicate this book with affection and respect."

"As we are, so our work is!" said Leighton in one of the most memorable of his Discourses; "and the moral effect of what we are will control the artist's work from the first touch of the brush or chisel to the last." "Believe me," he concludes, in a striking passage that may very fitly serve us, too, with a conclusion to these passages,

> "believe me, whatever of dignity, whatever of strength we have within us, will dignify and will make strong the labours of our hands; whatever littleness degrades our spirit will lessen them and drag them down. Whatever noble fire is in our hearts will burn also in our work, whatever purity is ours will also chasten and exalt it; for as we are, so our work is, and what we sow in our lives, that, beyond a doubt, we shall reap for good or for ill in the strengthening or defacing of whatever gifts have fallen to our lot."

It would be superfluous to quote from the elegiac tributes which appeared in the public press after Lord Leighton's death, and invidious to repeat certain unkind and unjust strictures which marred the otherwise unanimous note of appreciation. It is obvious that an artist with so strongly marked a personality must needs have been fettered by the very limits he himself had set. At one time, when a painter of eminence openly expressed his preference for Lord Leighton's unfinished work, and begged him to keep a certain picture as "a beautiful sketch," he replied: "No, I shall finish it, and probably, as you suggest, spoil it. To complete satisfactorily is what we painters live for. I am not a great painter, but I am always striving to finish my work up to my first conception."

There are many mansions in the city of Art, and if the one of Lord Leighton's building was not to the taste of all his contemporaries, the edifice can be left to await the final test of years. Fashions in taste change rapidly, and much of his finish that finds disfavour to-day may in time charm once again. A career overburdened by official honour was destined to provoke a certain amount of envious protest; but as a man, no voice has urged a word against his ideally perfect performance, not merely of his official duties, but of others which indeed were laid upon him by his position. These he obeyed without ostentation – almost without men's knowledge. His kindly help, by commendation or by commission given to young artists; his broad and tolerant view of work conceived in direct opposition to all he valued himself, was not hidden from his friends. "It is with a sense of amazement," a critic writes in a private letter, "that one afternoon after a protest that nothing he said was to be published, I heard him discuss the prospects and the works of our ultra-modern painters. Even in fields beyond his sympathy he picked out the chaff from the wheat, and was judicially accurate in his verdicts of the difference between 'tweedle-dum' and 'tweedle-dee,' both one would have said, entirely unknown to him."

In Lord Leighton British artists lost a truer friend than many of them suspected, one who wielded his power justly to all, and was more often on the side of progress than not, a power for reform that can never be estimated at its actual value, working within a highly conservative body, full of vested interests and prejudice – as is the habit of academies of Art and Literature abroad no less than at home. That Leighton, who controlled its destinies so long, was loyal to its true interests, and never forgot the institution with which he was associated so many years is evident from his last words: "Give my love to all at the Academy."

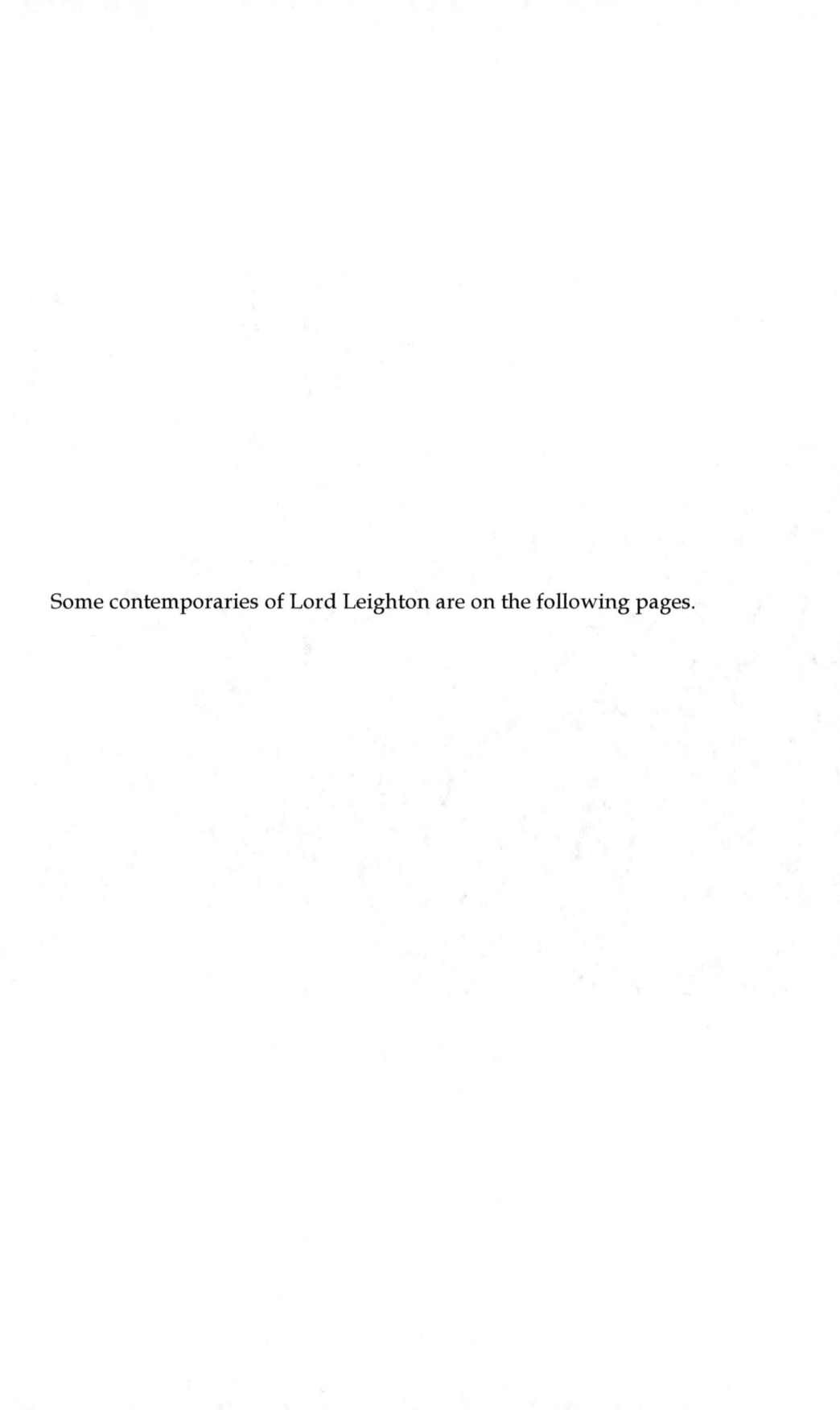

Some contemporaries of Lord Leighton are on the following pages.

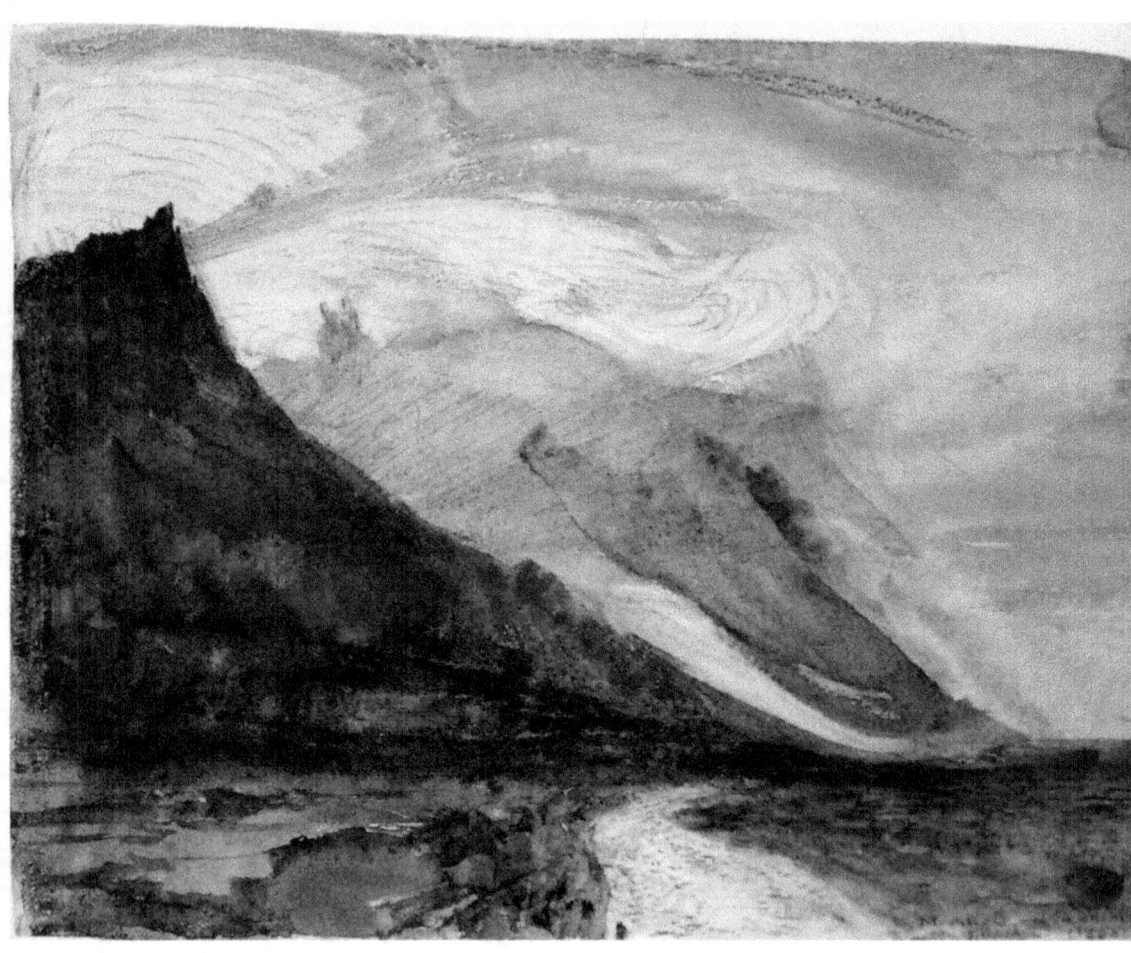

John Ruskin, Moonlight, Chamonix, 1888

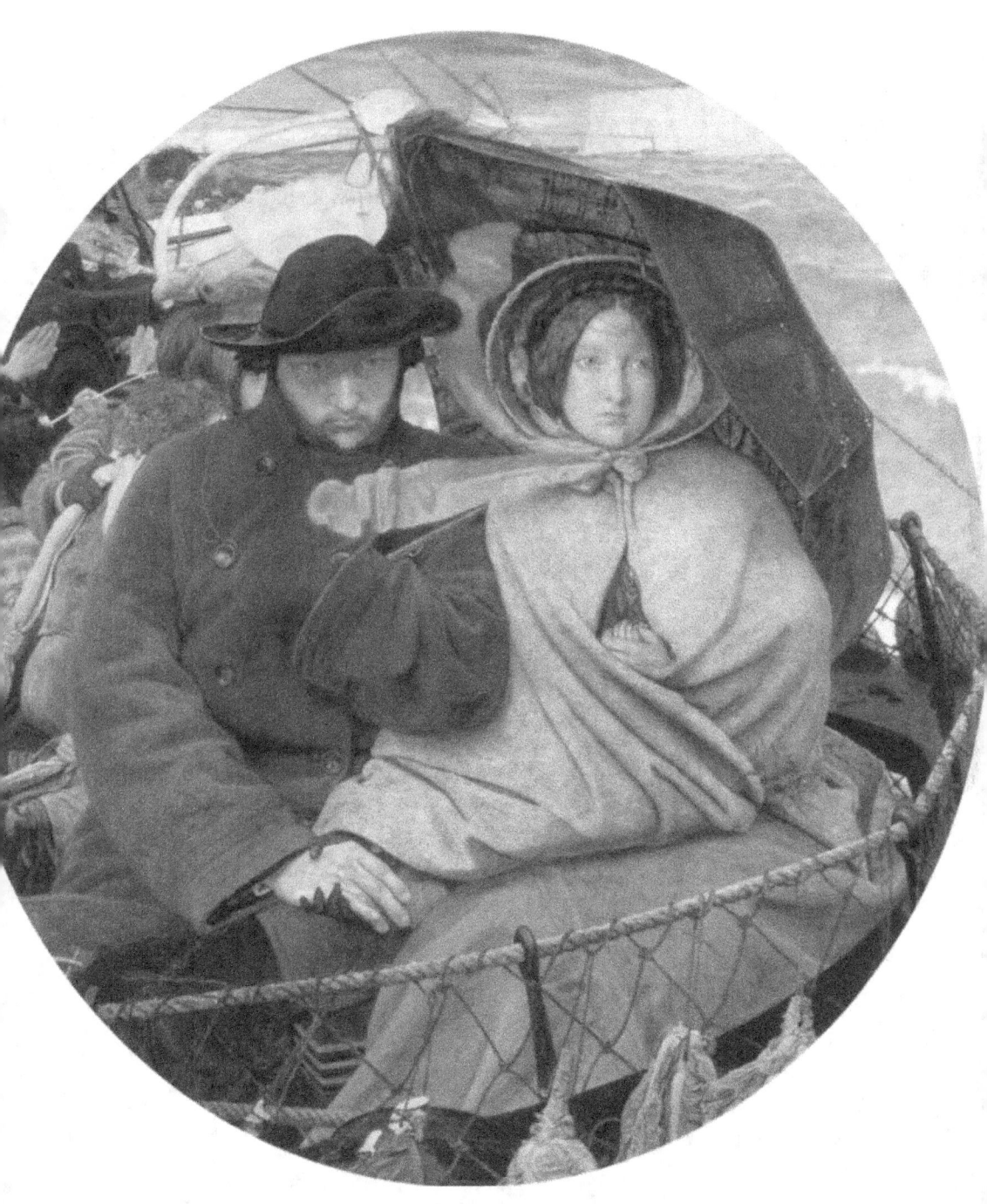

Ford Madox Brown, The Last of England, 1855,
Birmingham

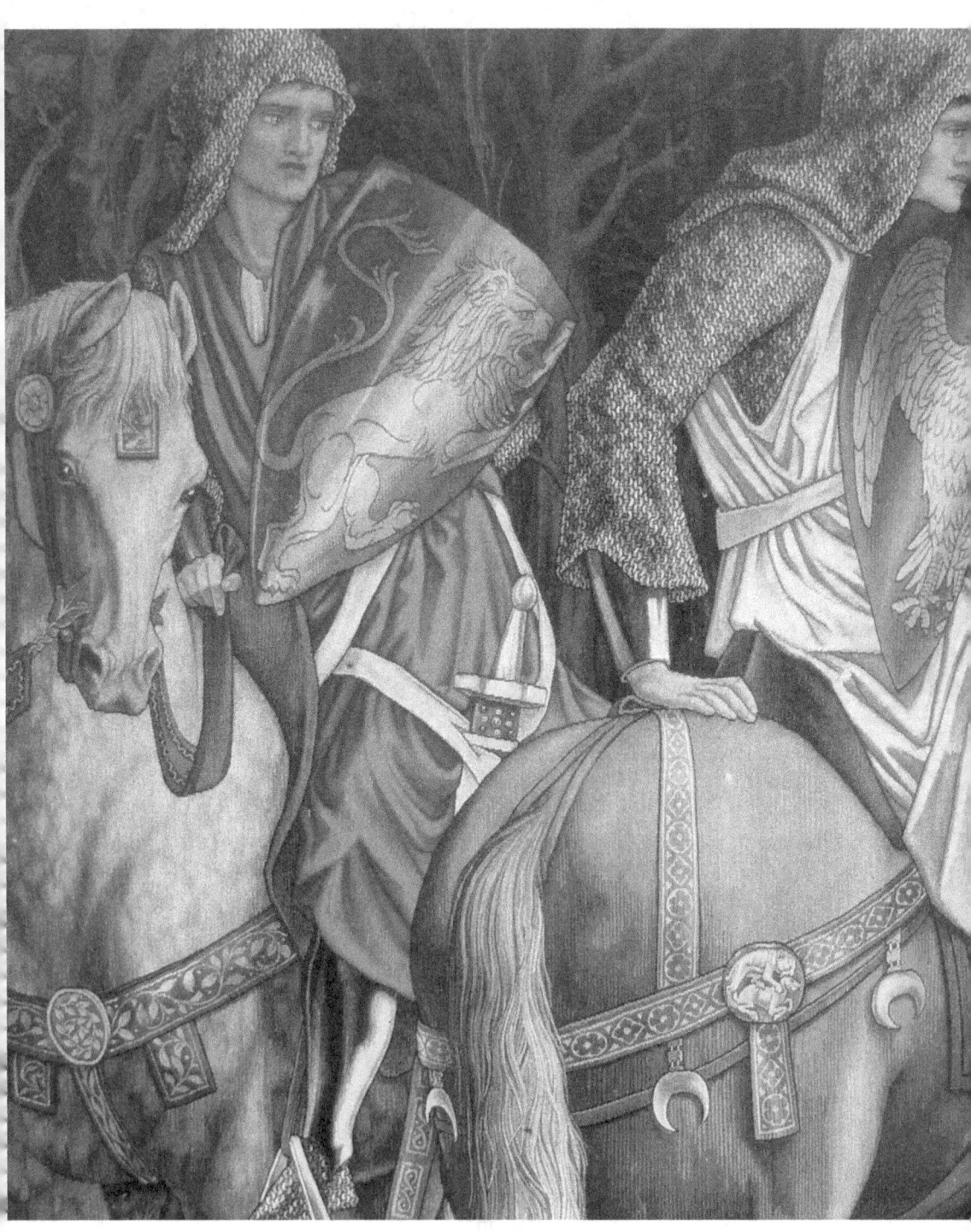

Edward Burne-Jones, The Fall of Lucifer, 1894, detail

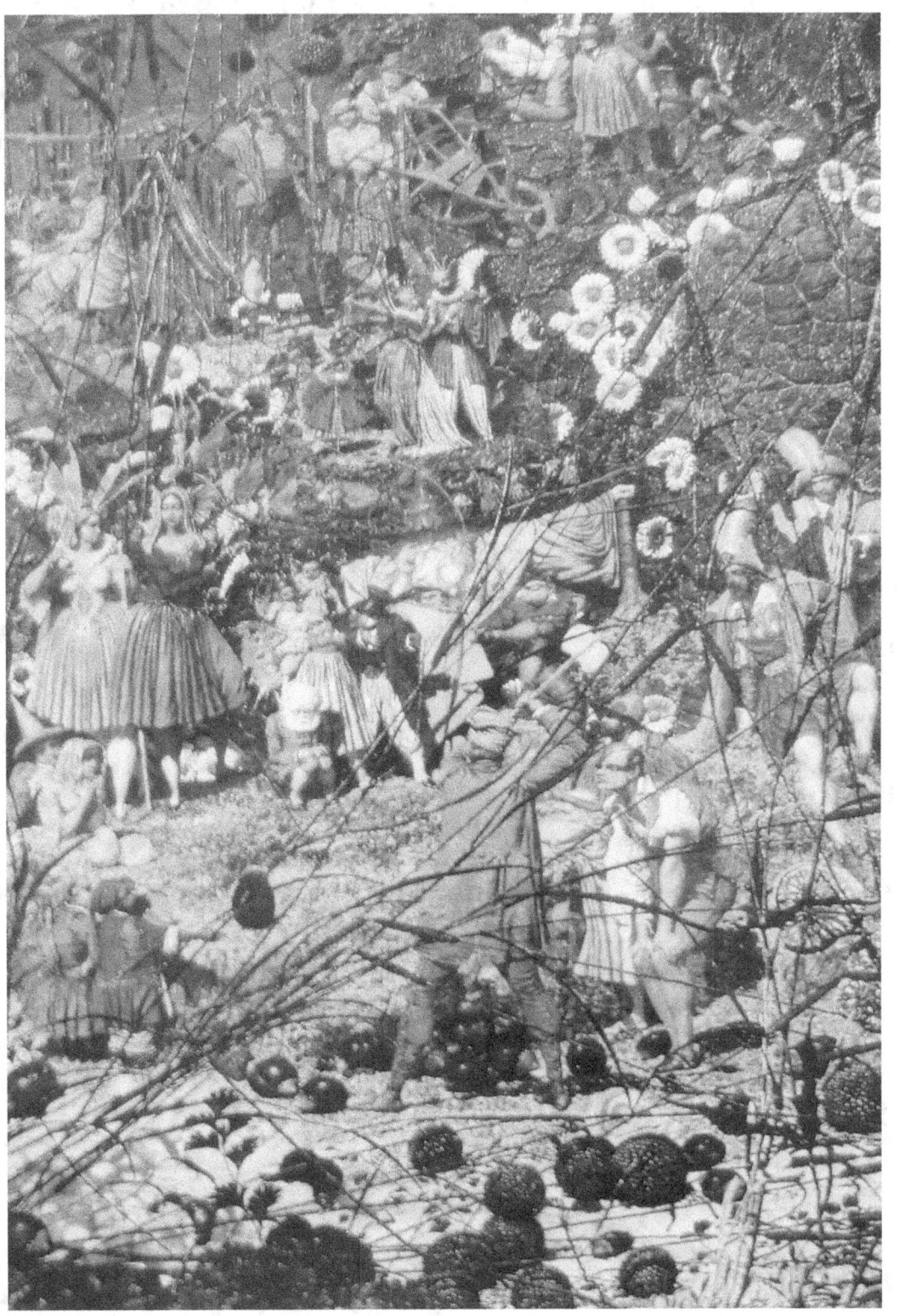

Richard Dadd, The Fairy-Feller's Master-Stroke, Tate, London

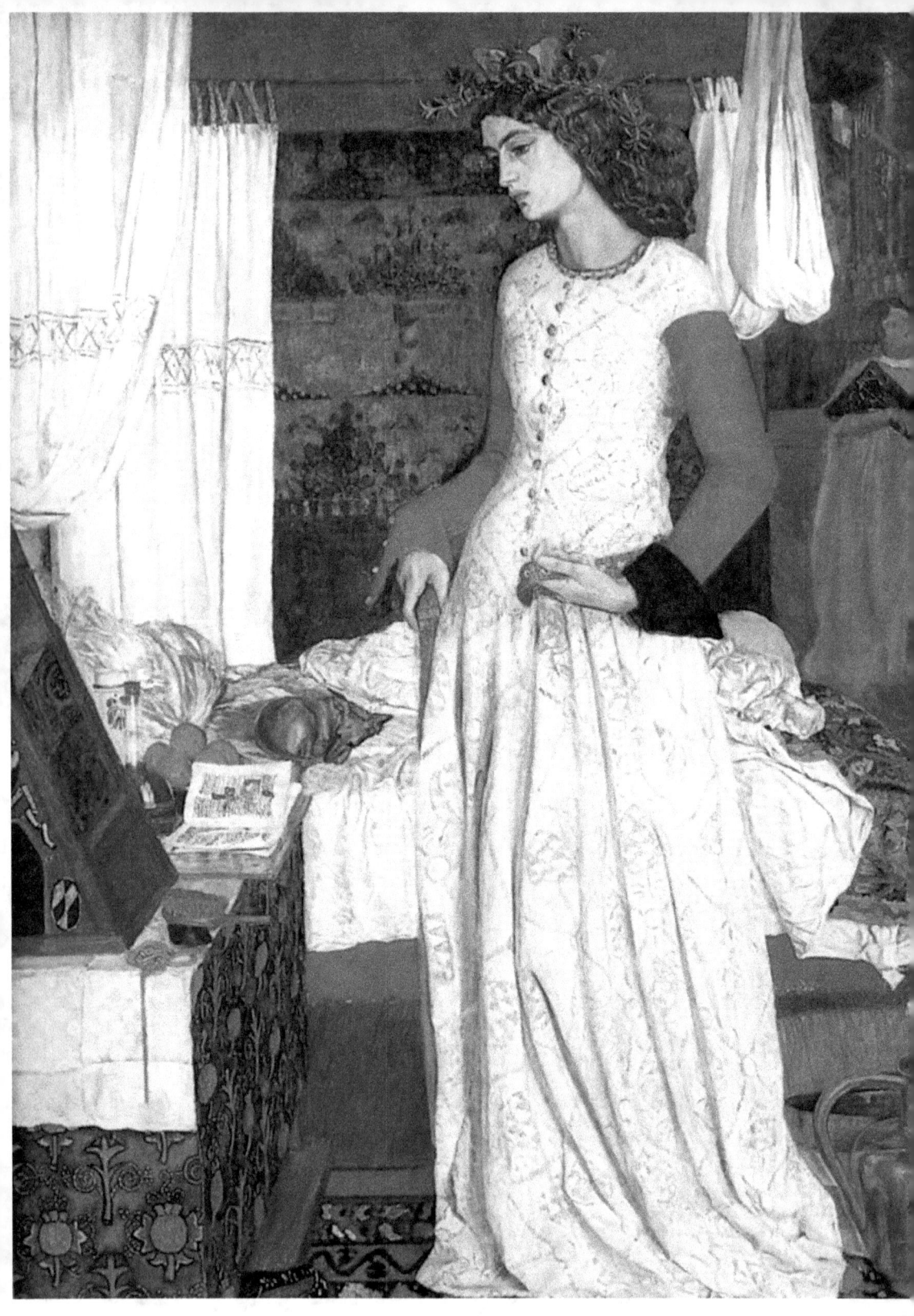

William Morris, La Belle Iseult, 1858, Tate Gallery

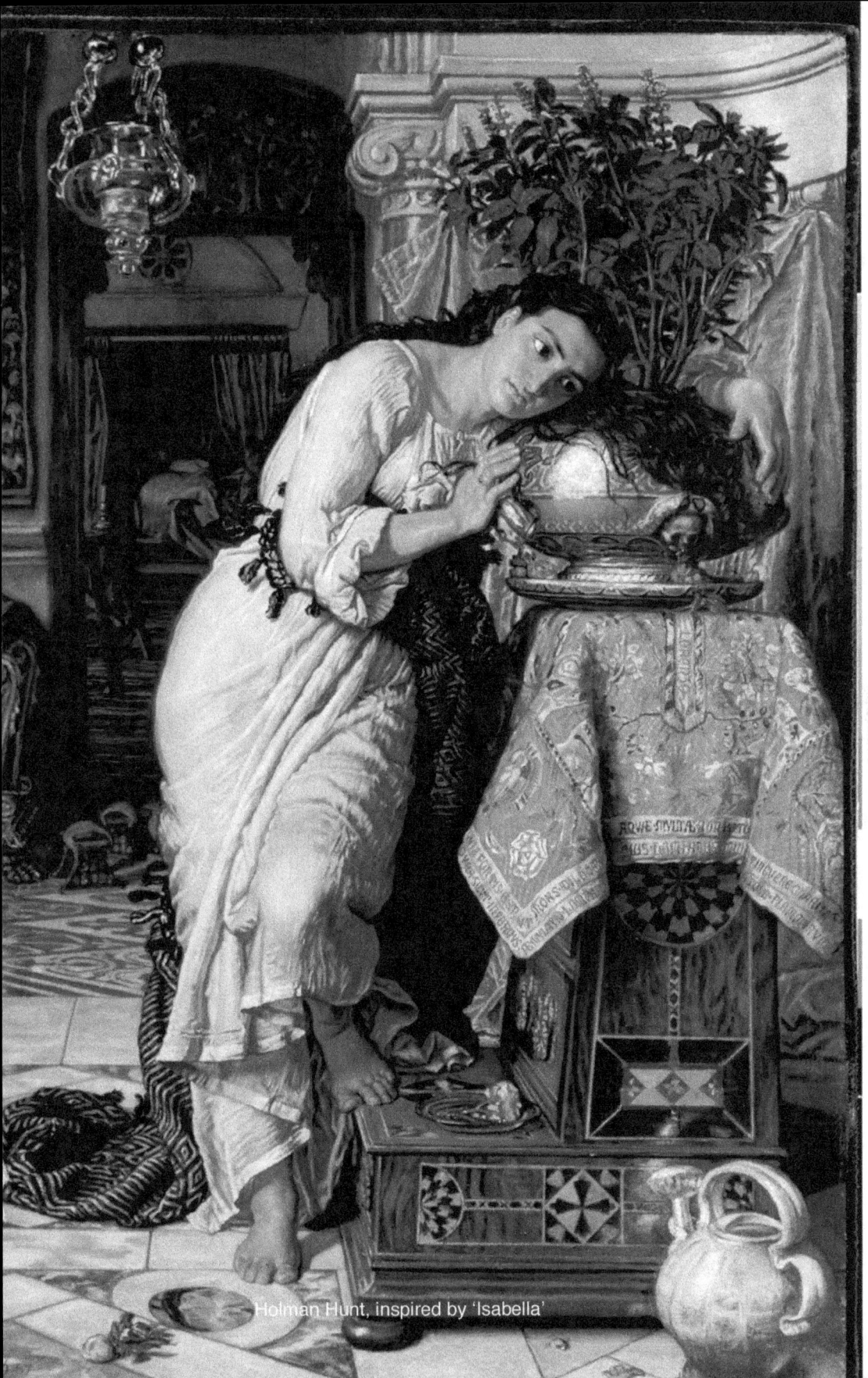
Holman Hunt, inspired by 'Isabella'

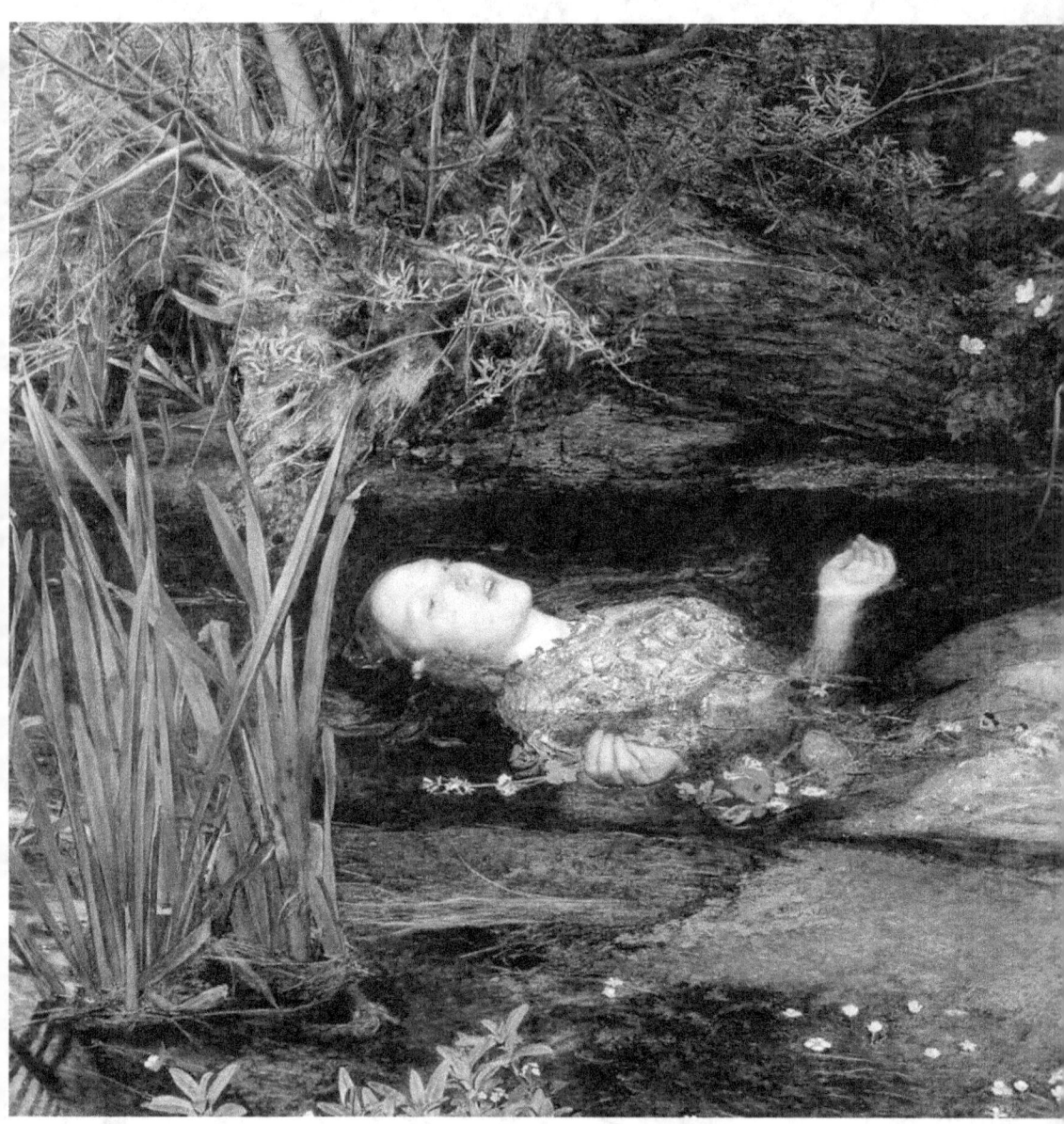

John Everett Millais, Ophelia.

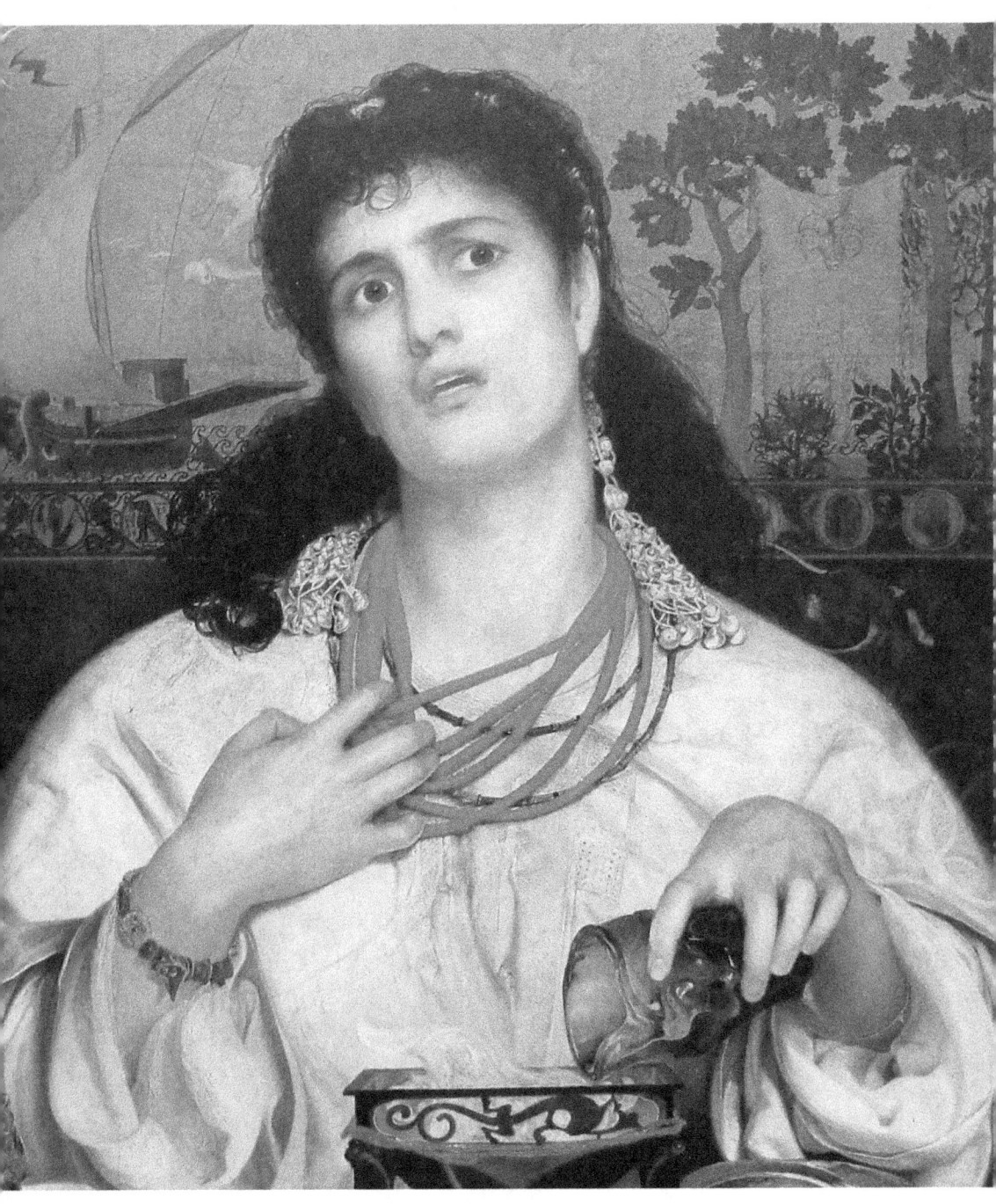

Frederick Sandys, Medea, 1868

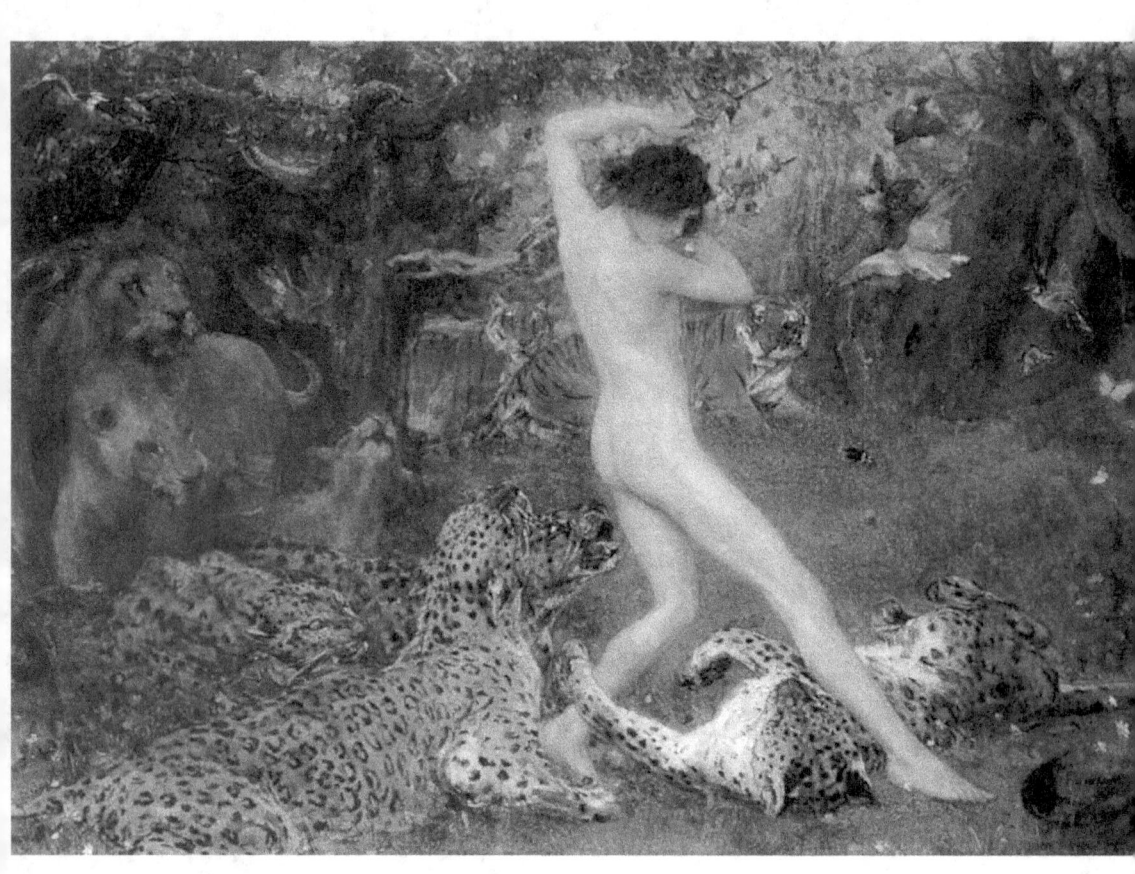

John Macallan Swan, Orpheus, 1896

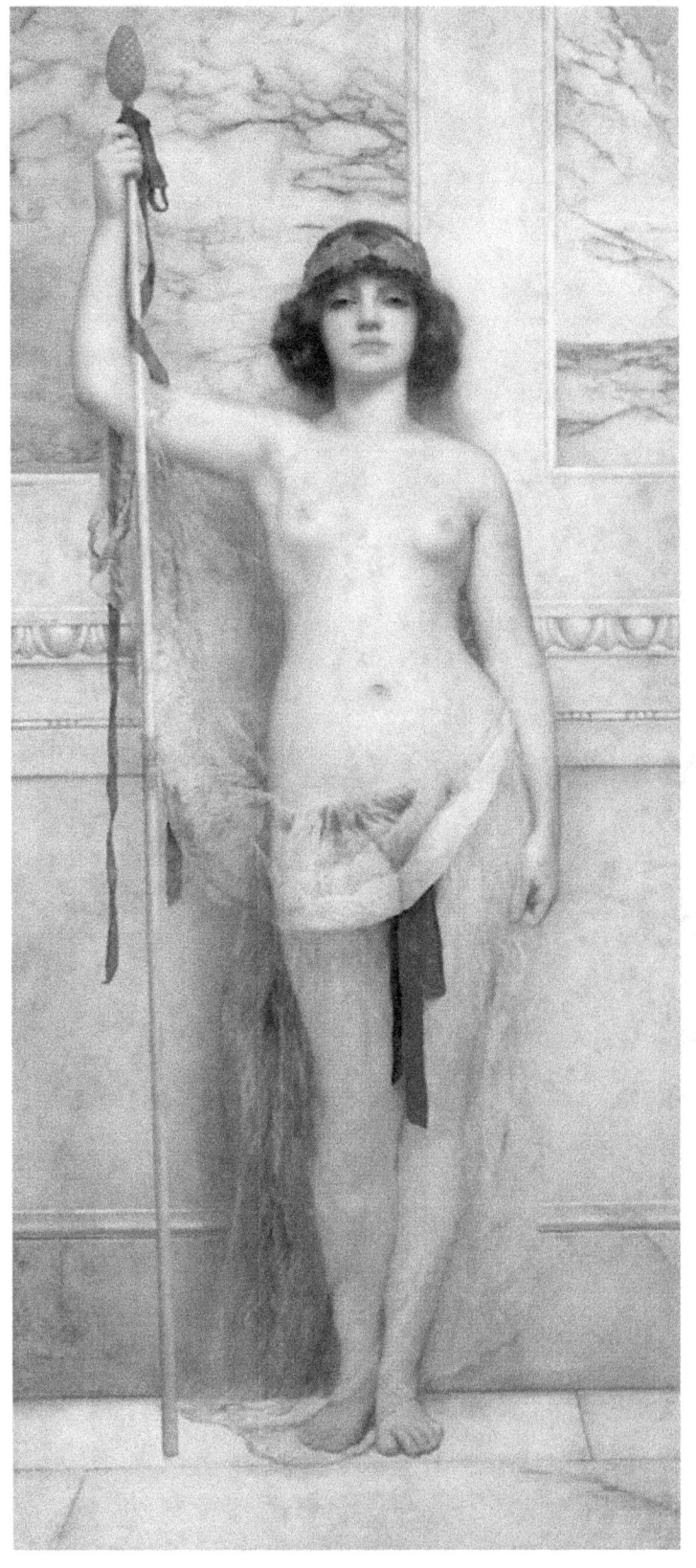

John Godward, A Priestess, 1893

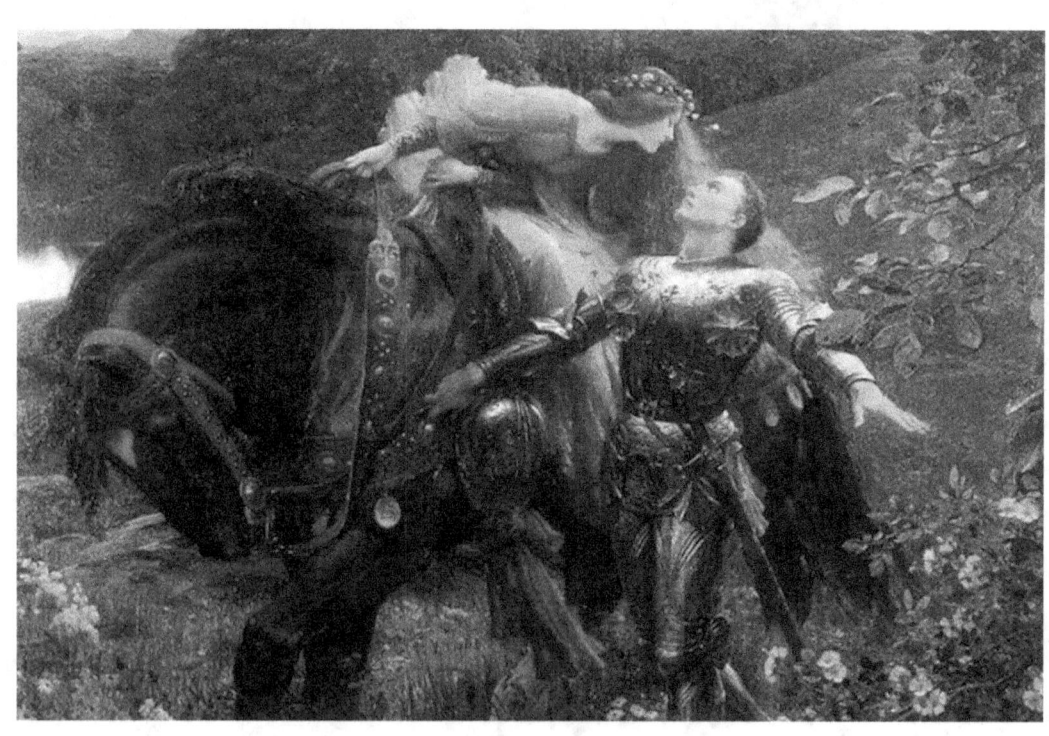

Sir Francis Dicksee, 'La Belle Dame Sans Merci'

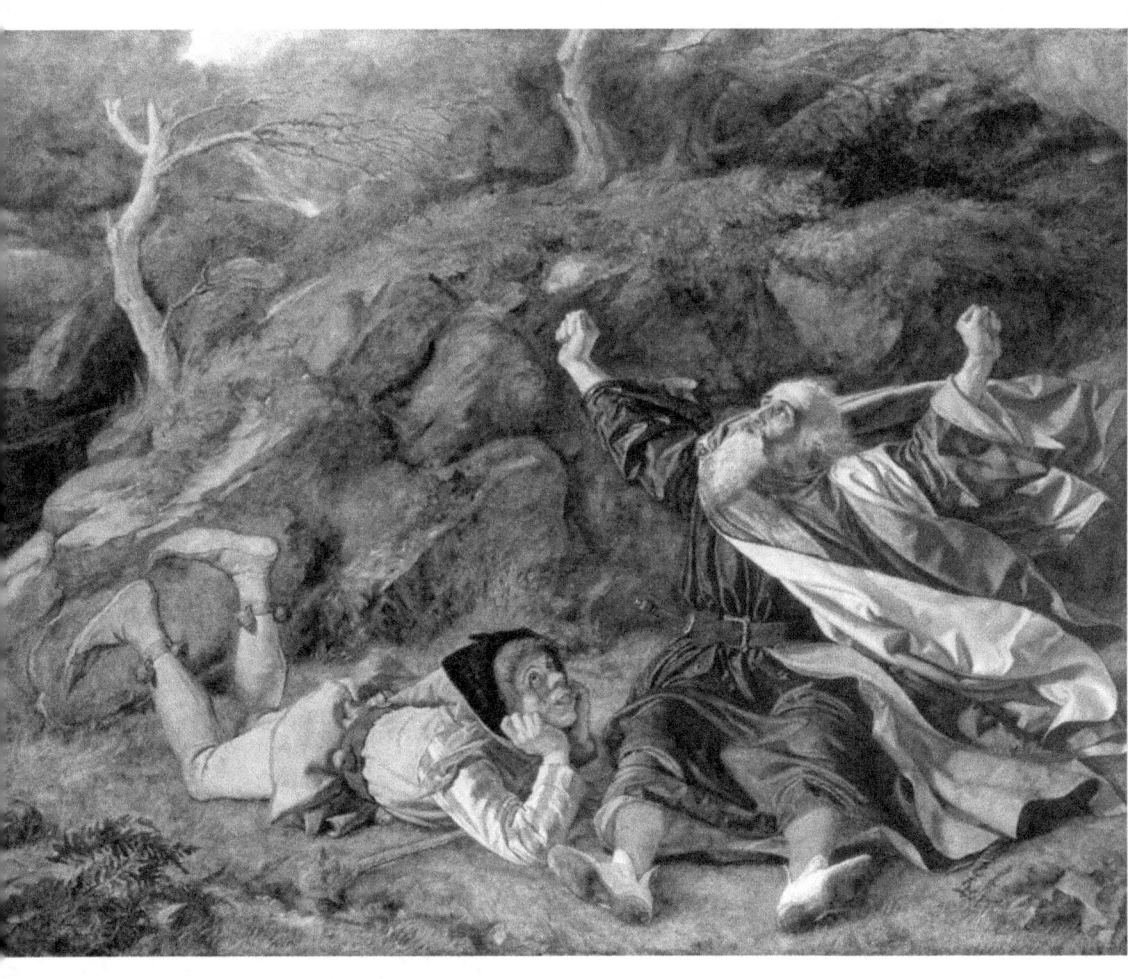

William Dyce, King Lear and the Fool In the Storm, 1851, Edinburgh

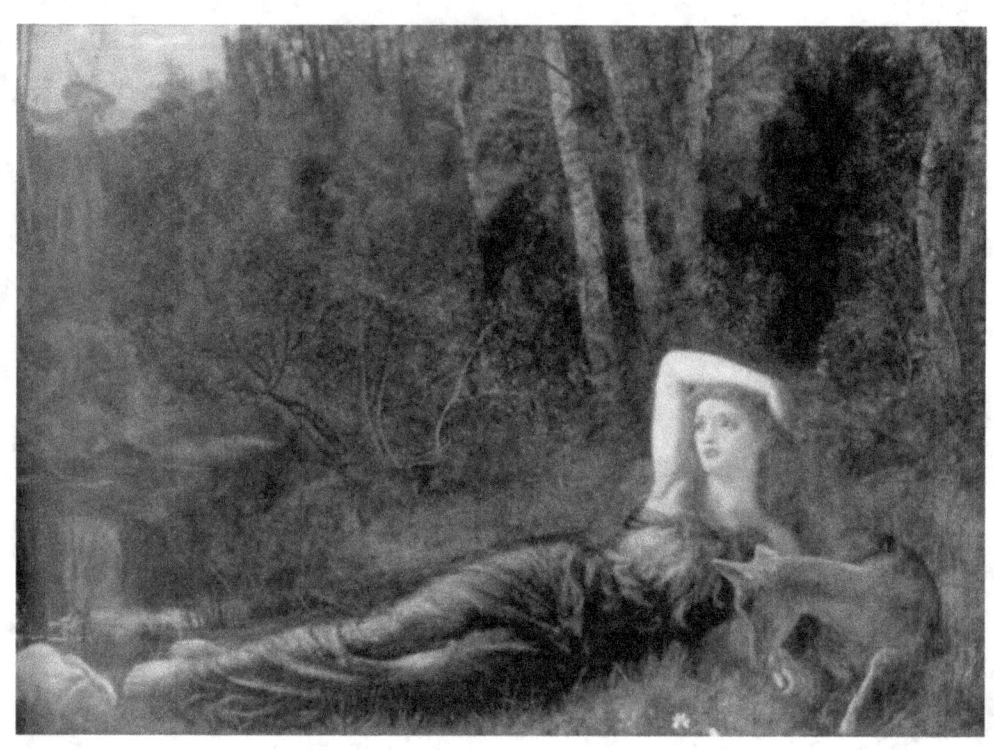

Arthur Hughes, Endymion

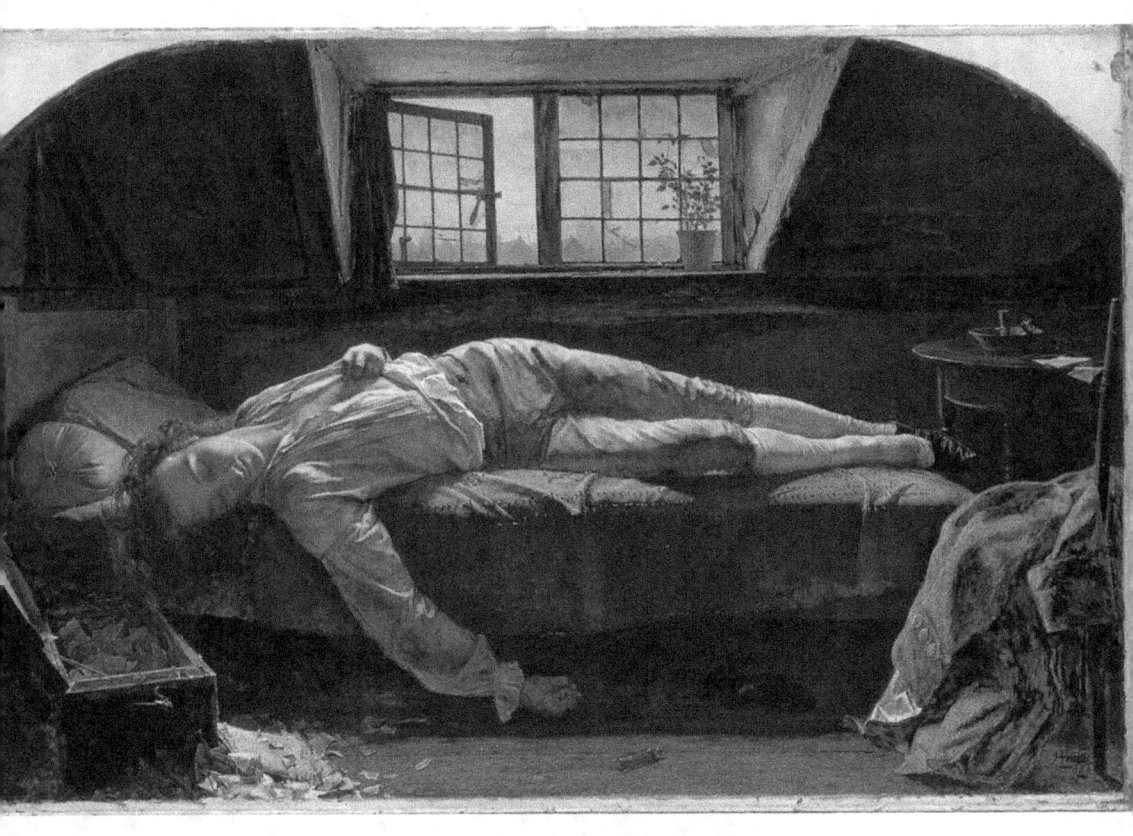

Henry Wallis, Chatterton, 1856, Tate Britain

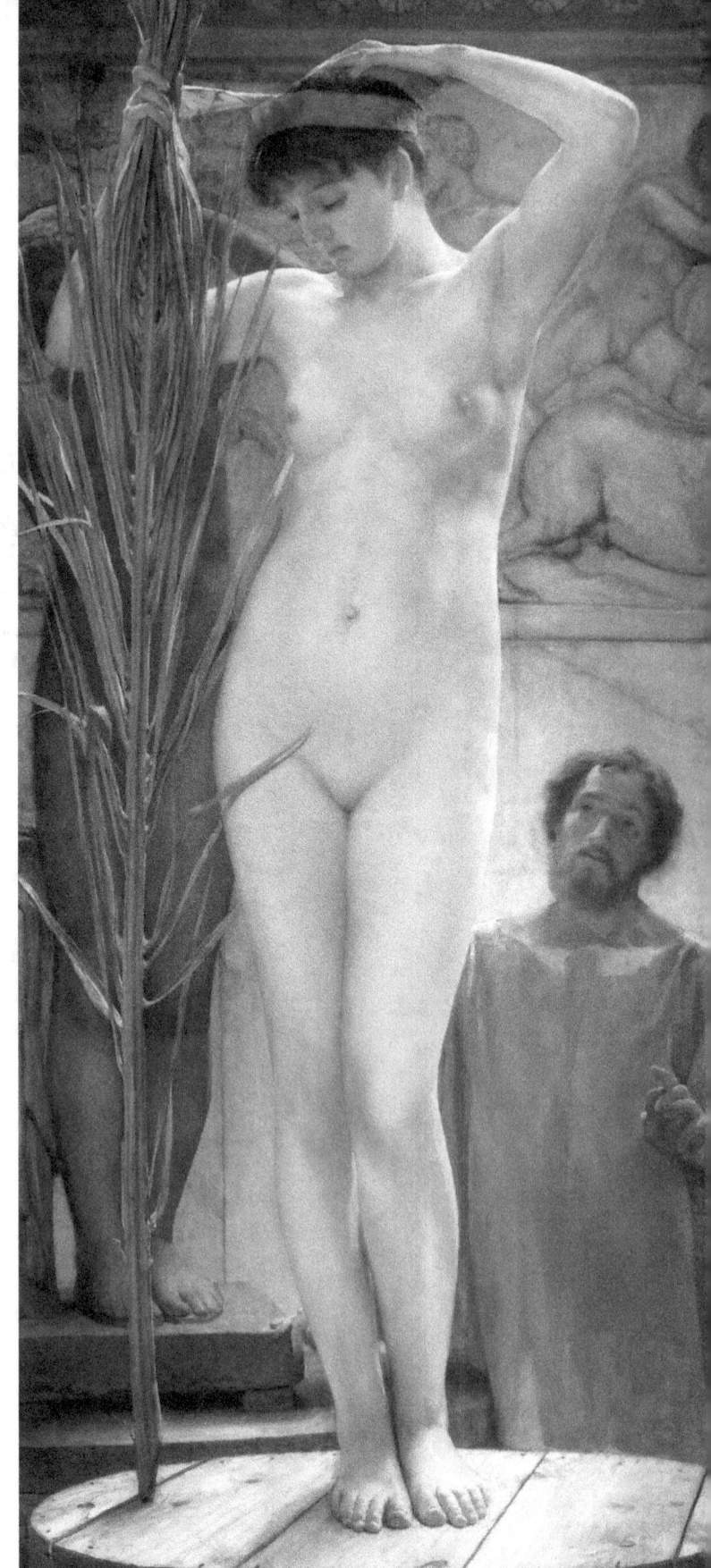

Lawrence
Alma-Tadema,
A Sculptor's Model,
1877, private
collection

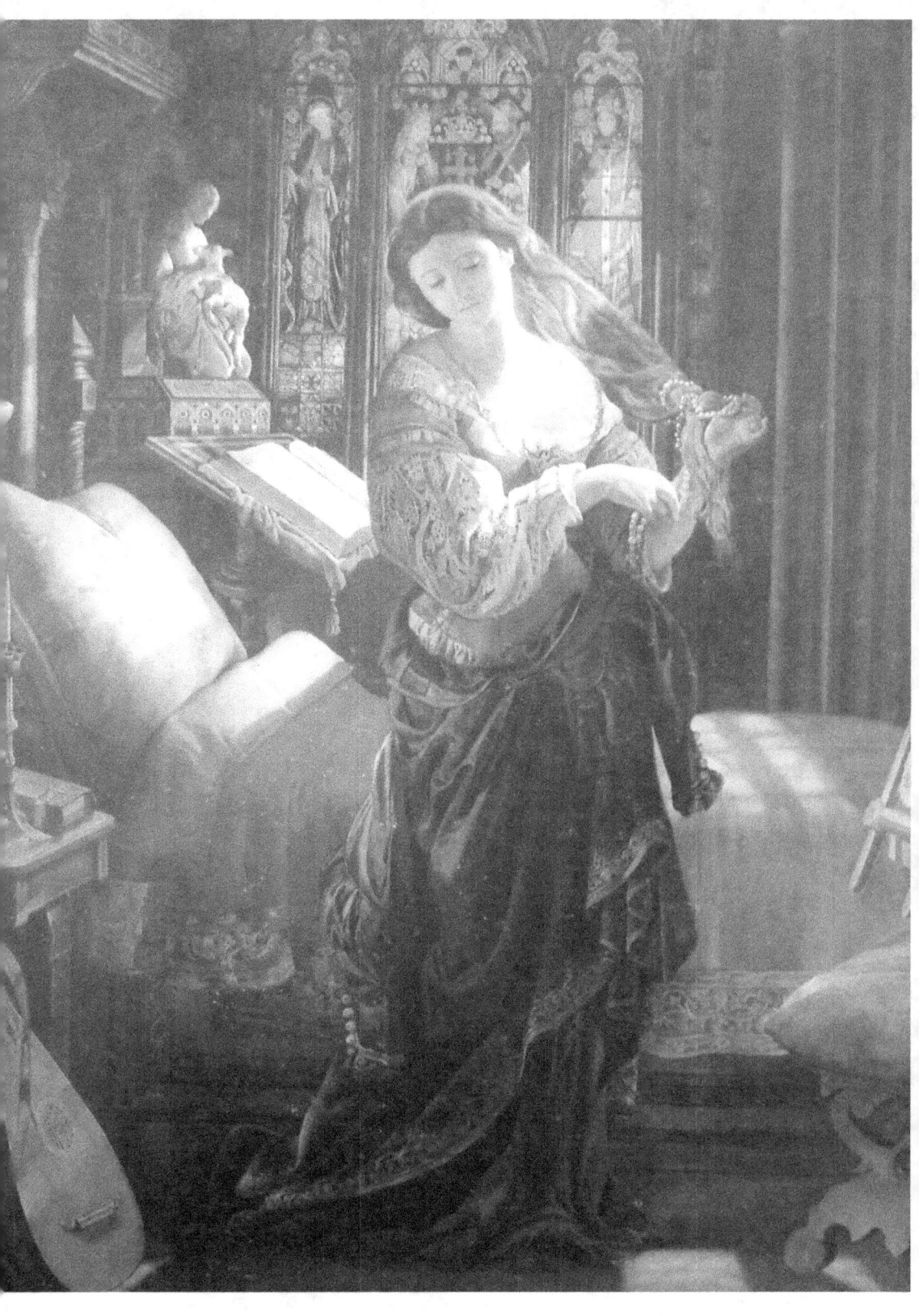

Daniel Maclise, Madeline After Prayer, 1868, Walker Art Gallery

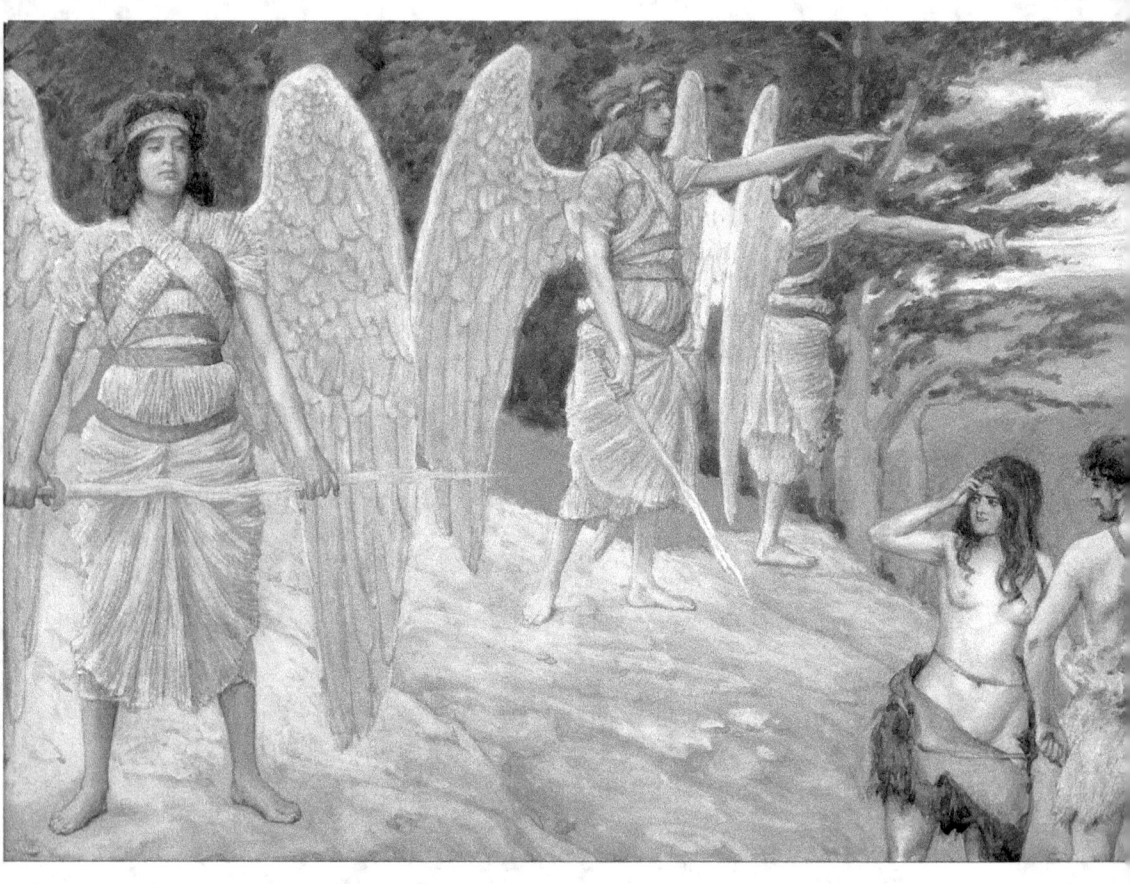

James Tissot, Adam and Eve Driven From Paradise, Jewish Museum, NYC

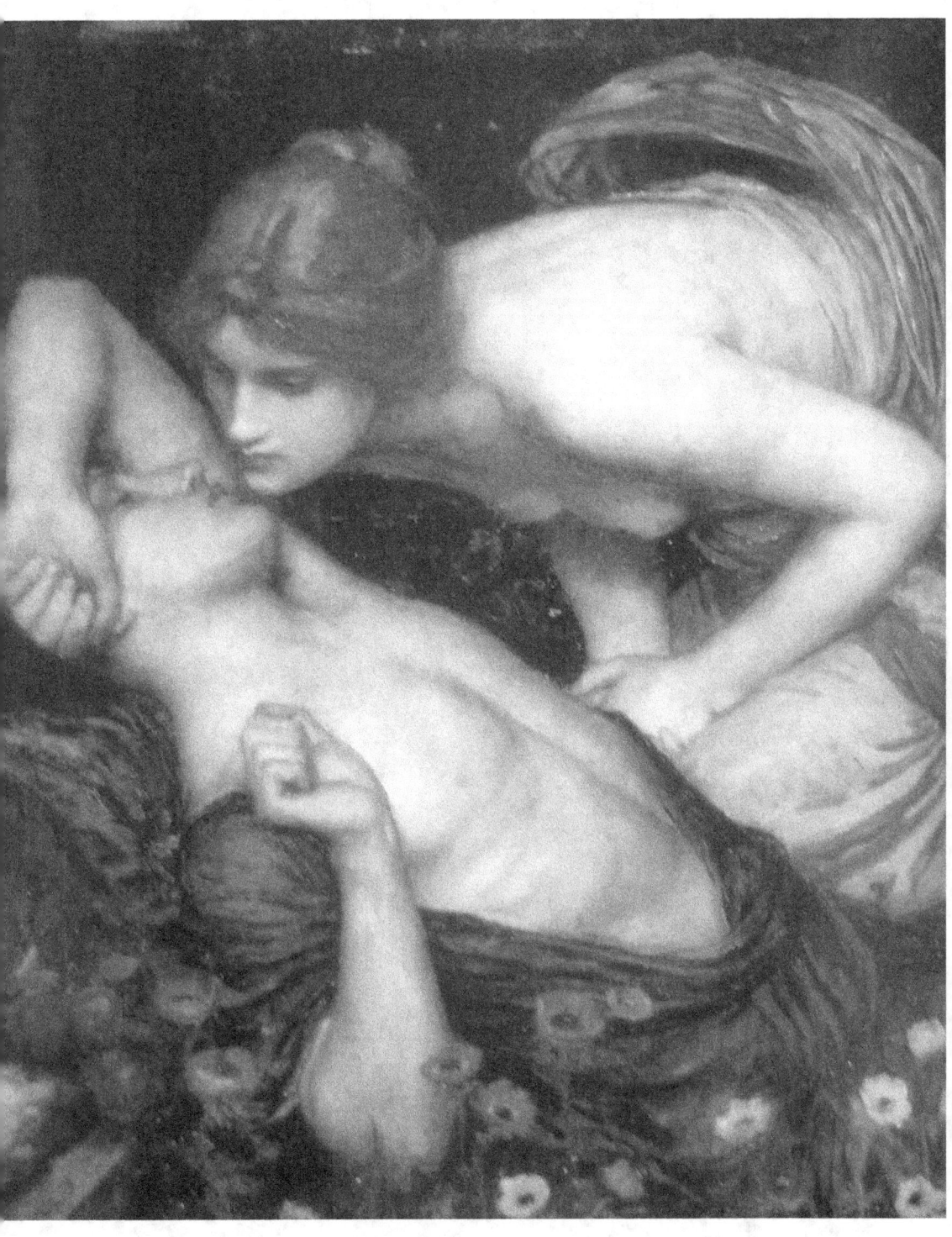

John William Waterhouse, The Awakening of Adonis, 1899, detail

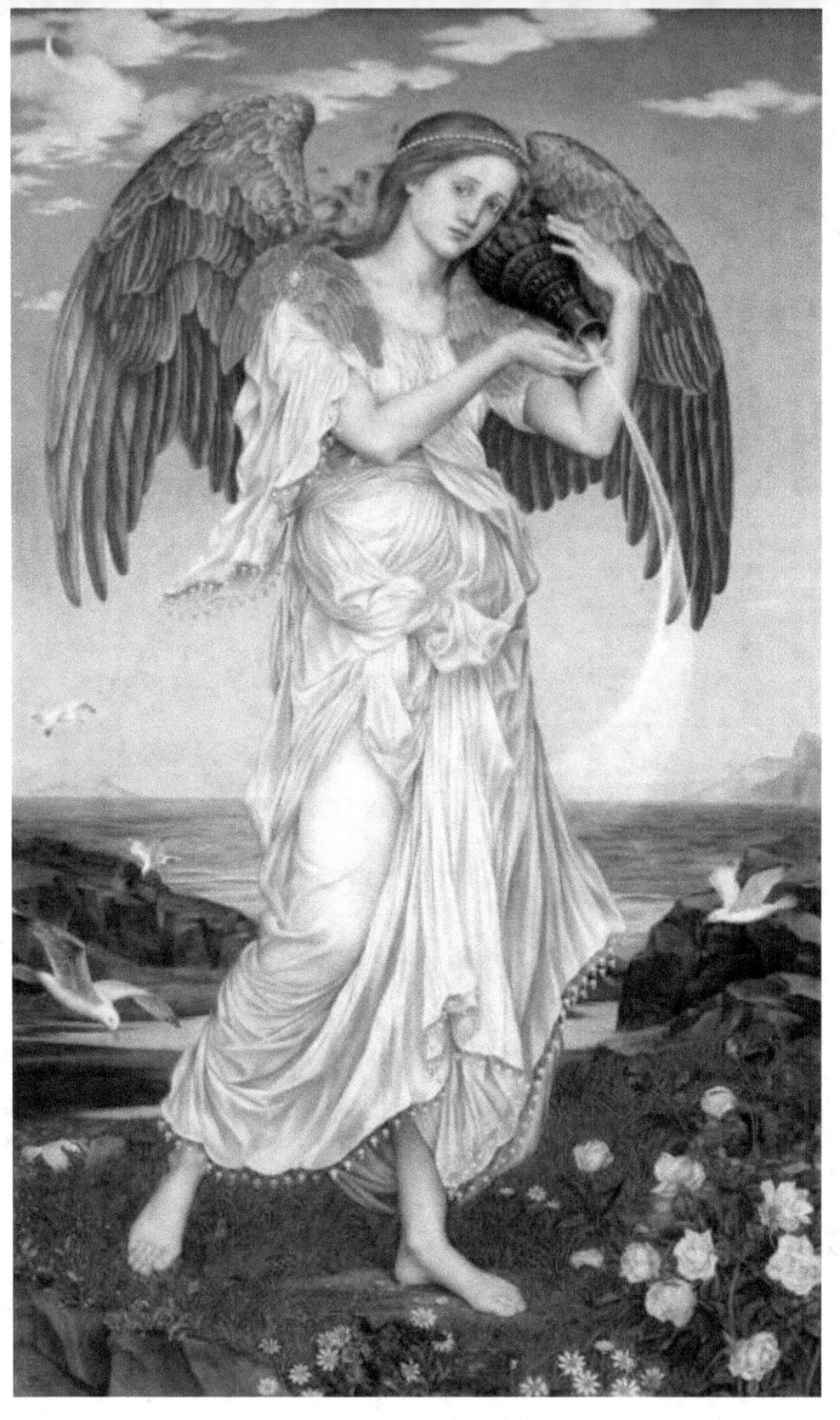

Evelyn de Morgan, Eos, 1895, Columbus, Ohio

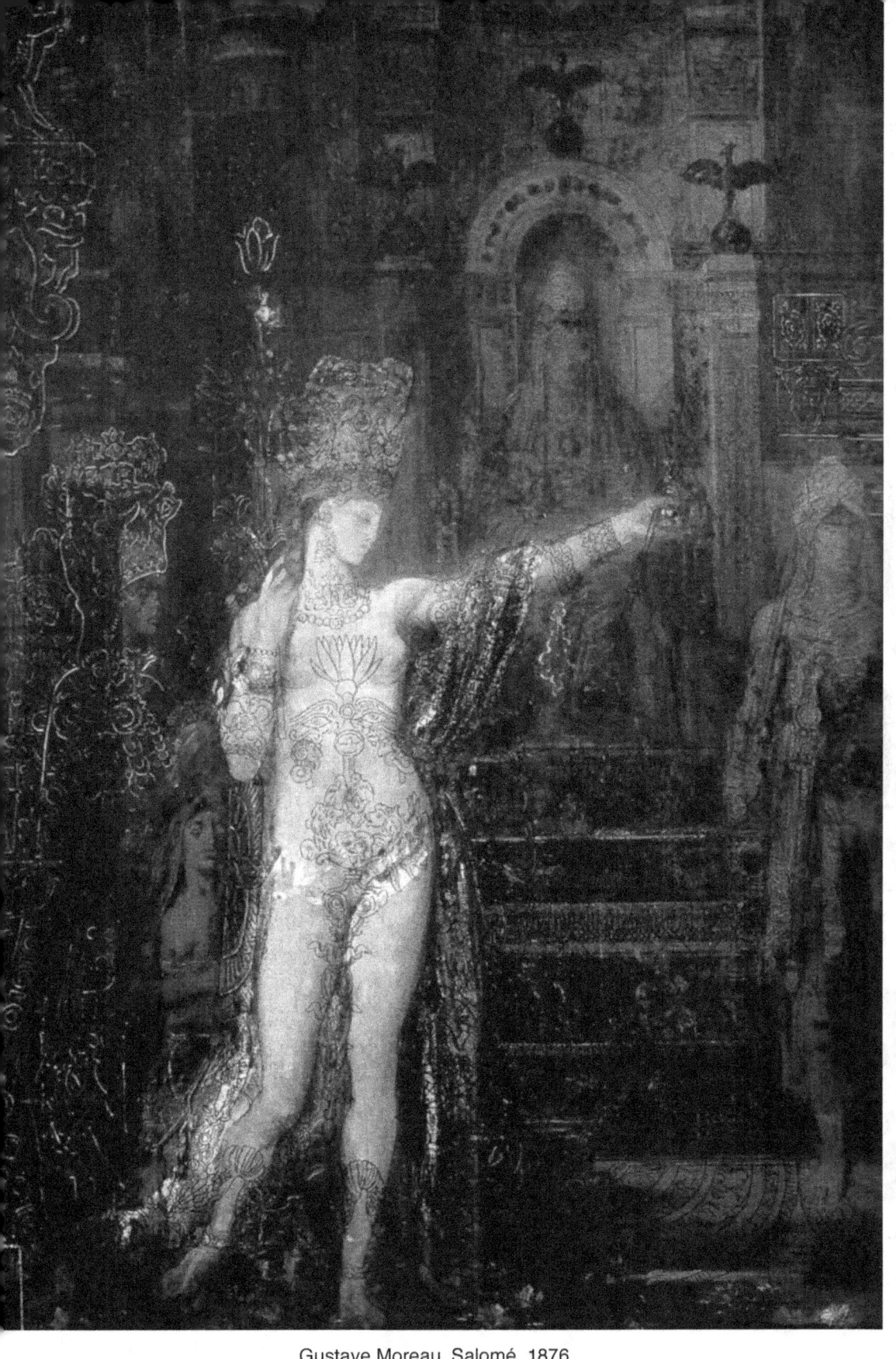

Gustave Moreau, Salomé, 1876

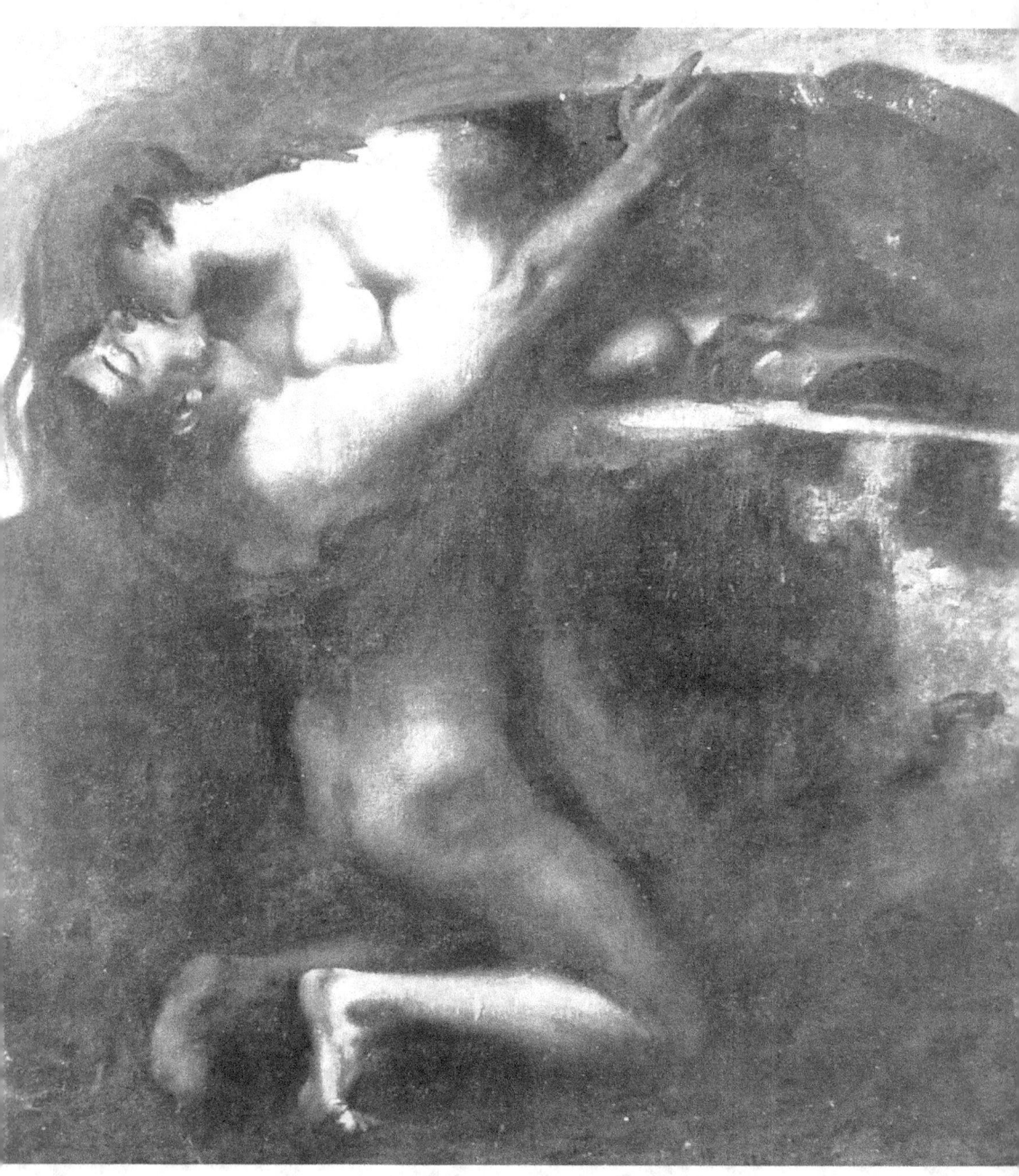

Franz von Stuck, Sphinx

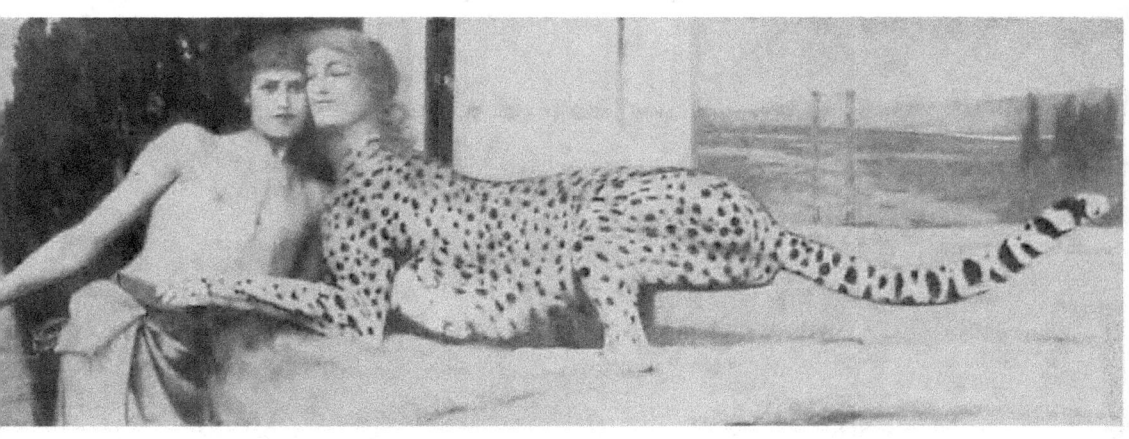

Fernand Knopff, The Caresses of the Sphinx, 1896, Brussels

APPENDIX I

List of Principal Works

With date and place of exhibition

1850 (*circa*).
*Cimabue finding Giotto in the Fields of Florence. [15]
Steinle Institute (Frankfort).

1850.
The Duel between Romeo and Tybalt.

1851 (*circa*).
The Death of Brunelleschi.
Steinle Institute.

1851.
[Early Portrait of Leighton by himself.]

1852.
*A Persian Pedlar.
[Buffalmacco, the Painter. A humorous subject, taken from Vasari, was undertaken about this date.]

1853.

Portrait of Miss Laing (Lady Nias).

1855.

*Cimabue's Celebrated Madonna is carried in procession through the streets of Florence.

In front of the Madonna, and crowned with laurels, walks Cimabue himself, with his pupil Giotto; behind it, Arnolfo di Lapo, Gaddo Gaddi, Andrea Tafi, Nicola Pisano, Buffalmacco and Simone Memmi; in the corner, Dante.

R.A. [16]

The Reconciliation of the Montagues and Capulets over the dead bodies of Romeo and Juliet.

Paris International Exhibition. [17]

1856.

The Triumph of Music.

"Orpheus, by the power of his art, redeems his wife from Hades."

R.A.

1857.

*Salome, the daughter of Herodias.

1858.

*The Mermaid (The Fisherman and the Syren).

(From a ballad by Goethe.)

R.A.

 "Half drew she him,
Half sunk he in,
And never more was seen."

"Count Paris, accompanied by Friar Lawrence and a band of

✛ 157

musicians, comes to the house of the Capulets, to claim his bride: he finds Juliet stretched apparently lifeless on her bed." – *Romeo and Juliet*, act IV., sc. 5.

R.A.

Reminiscence of Algiers.

S.S.

These were,

[A Subject from Keats's Hymn to Pan,] *in the first book of "Endymion," a figure of Pan*

under a fig-tree, with the inscription,

"O thou, to whom
Broad-leaved fig-trees even now foredoom
Their ripen'd fruitage;"

and the other,

[A Pendant to the "Pan,"] *the figure of a nude nymph about to bathe, with a little Cupid loosening her sandal.*

1859.

Sunny Hours.

R.A.

*Roman Lady (La Nanna).

R.A.

*Nanna (Pavonia).

R.A.

Samson and Delilah.

S.S.

1860.

Capri – Sunrise.

R.A.

1861.

*Portrait of Mrs. Sutherland Orr. [Mrs. S. O., a portrait.]
R.A.
*Portrait of John Hanson Walker, Esq.
Paolo e Francesca.

"Ma solo un punto fu quel che ci vinse
Quando legemmo il disiato riso
Esser baciato da cotanto amante,
Questi, che mai da me non fia diviso,
La bocca mi baciò tutto tremante:
Galeotto fu'l libro e chi lo scrisse:
Quel giorno più non vi legemmo avante."

R.A.
A Dream.

... "Not yet – not yet –
Still there is trial for thee, still the lot
To bear (the Father wills it) strife and care;
With this sweet consciousness in balance set
Against the world, to soothe thy suffering there
Thy Lord rejects thee not.
Such tender words awoke me hopeful, shriven
To life on earth again from dream of heaven."

R.A.
Lieder ohne Worte.
R.A.
J. A. A Study.
R.A.
Capri – Paganos.
R.A.

1862.
Odalisque.

R.A.

*The Star of Bethlehem.

One of the Magi, from the terrace of his house, stands looking at the star in the East; the lower part of the

picture indicates a road, which he may be supposed just to have left.

R.A.

Sisters.

R.A.

*Michael Angelo Nursing His Dying Servant.

R.A.

Duett.

R.A.

Sea Echoes.

R.A.

Rustic Music.

1863.

Jezebel and Ahab, having caused Naboth to be put to death, go down to take possession of his vineyard; they are met at the entrance by Elijah the Tishbite:

"Hast thou killed, and also taken possession?"

R.A.

*Eucharis. (A Girl with a Basket of Fruit.)

R.A.

A Girl Feeding Peacocks.

R.A.

An Italian Crossbow-man.

R.A.

1864.

Dante at Verona.

R.A.

*Orpheus and Eurydice.

"But give them me – the mouth, the eyes, – the brow –
Let them once more absorb me! One look now
Will lap me round for ever, not to pass
Out of its light, though darkness lie beyond!
Hold me but safe again within the bond
Of one immortal look! All woe that was,
Forgotten, and all terror that may be,
Defied – no past is mine, no future! look at me!"
Robert Browning: *A Fragment*.

R.A.
*Golden Hours.
R.A.
*Portrait of the Late Miss Lavinia I'Anson. (Circular)

1865.
*David.
"Oh that I had wings like a dove! for then would I fly away
and be at rest." *Psalm* lv.
R.A.
Mother and Child.
R.A.
Widow's Prayer.
R.A.
Helen of Troy.

"Thus as she spoke, in Helen's breast arose
Fond recollections of her former lord,
Her home, and parents; o'er her head she threw
A snowy veil; and shedding tender tears
She issued forth not unaccompanied;
For with her went fair Æthra, Pittheus' child.
And stag-eyed Clymene, her maidens twain.

They quickly at the Scæan gate arrived."

R.A.
In St. Mark's.
R.A.

1866.
Painter's Honeymoon.
R.A.
Portrait of Mrs. James Guthrie.
R.A.
Syracusan Bride Leading Wild Beasts in Procession to the Temple of Diana.
(Suggested by a passage in the second Idyll of Theocritus.)
"And for her, then, many other wild beasts were going in procession round about, and among them a lioness."
R.A.
The Wise and Foolish Virgins. (Fresco in Lyndhurst Church.)

1867.
*Pastoral.
R.A.
*Greek Girl Dancing. (Spanish Dancing Girl: Cadiz in the old times.)
R.A.
Knuckle-bone Player.
R.A.
*Roman Mother.
R.A.
*Venus Disrobing for the Bath.
R.A.
*Portrait of Mrs. John Hanson Walker.

1868.
Jonathan's Token To David.

"And it came to pass in the morning, that Jonathan went out into the field at the time appointed by David, and a little lad with him."

R.A.

*Portrait of Mrs. Frederick P. Cockerell.

R.A.

*Portrait of John Martineau, Esq.

*Ariadne Abandoned by Theseus; Ariadne watches for his return; Artemis releases her by death.

R.A.

*Acme and Septimius. (Circular)

"Then bending gently back her head
With that sweet mouth, so rosy red,
Upon his eyes she dropped a kiss,
Intoxicating him with bliss."
Catullus (Theodore Martin's translation).

R.A.

*Actæa, the Nymph of the Shore.

R.A.

1869.

*St. Jerome. (Diploma work, deposited in the Academy on his election as an Academician.)

R.A.

*Dædalus and Icarus.

R.A.

*Electra at the Tomb of Agamemnon.

R.A.

*Helios and Rhodos.

R.A.

1870.

A Nile Woman.

R.A.

Study.

S.S.

1871.

*Hercules Wrestling with Death for the Body of Alcestis.

R.A.

Greek Girls Picking up Pebbles by the Shore of the Sea.

R.A.

*Cleoboulos instructing his daughter Cleobouline.

R.A.

View of Assiout(?) (*A sketch.*)

S.S.

Sunrise at Longsor. (*A sketch.*)

S.S.

View of the Red Mountains near Cairo. (*A sketch.*)

S.S.

1872.

*After Vespers.

R.A.

*Summer Moon. (Guildhall, 1890.)

R.A.

Portrait of the Right Hon. Edward Ryan, Secretary of the Dilettanti Society, for which the picture was painted. (S.P.P., 1893.)

R.A.

A Condottiere.

R.A.

*The Industrial Arts of War at the International Exhibition at South Kensington. (Monochrome, 76 x 177 in.)

The Captive.

S.S.

An Arab Café, Algiers.

S.S.

1873.

*Weaving the Wreath. (Guildhall, 1895.)

R.A.

Moretta. (Guildhall, 1894.)

R.A.

*The Industrial Arts of Peace. (Monochrome)

R.A.

A Roman.

S.S.

Vittoria.

S.S.

1874.

*Moorish Garden: a dream of Granada. (Guildhall, 1895.)

R.A.

Old Damascus: Jews' Quarter.

R.A.

*Antique Juggling Girl. (Guildhall, 1892.)

R.A.

Clytemnestra from the battlements of Argos watches for the beacon fires which are to announce the return of Agamemnon.

R.A.

Annarella, Ana Capri.

D.G.

Rubinella, Capri.

D.G.

Lemon Tree, Capri.

D.G.

West Court of Palazzo, Venice.

D.G.

1875.

*Portion of the Interior of the Grand Mosque Of Damascus.

R.A.

*Portrait of Mrs. H. E. Gordon
R.A.
*Little Fatima.
R.A.
Venetian Girl.
R.A.
*Egyptian Slinger. (Eastern Slinger Scaring Birds in Harvest-time: Moonrise.) (Guildhall, 1890.)
R.A.
Florentine Youth.
S.S.
Ruined Mosque in Damascus.
S.S.

1876.
*Portrait of Sir Richard Francis Burton, K.C.M.G.
(Portrait of Capt. Richard Burton, H.M. Consul at Trieste). (Paris, 1878; Melbourne, 1888;
S.P.P., 1892.)
R.A.
*The Daphnephoria.
A triumphal procession held every ninth year at Thebes, in honour of Apollo and to commemorate a
victory of the Thebans over the Æolians of Arne. (See Proclus, "Chrestomath," p. 11.)
R.A.
Teresina.
R.A.
Paolo.
R.A.

1877.
*Music Lesson. (Paris, 1878.)
R.A.
*Portrait of Miss Mabel Mills (The Hon. Mrs. Grenfell).

R.A.

*An Athlete strangling a Python. [18] Bronze. (Paris, 1878.)

R.A.

*Portrait of H. E. Gordon.

G.G.

An Italian Girl.

G.G.

*Study. (A little girl with fair hair, in a pink robe.) (24 x 28 in.)

R.A.

A Study.

G.G.

1878.

*Nausicaa. (Guildhall, 1896.)

R.A.

Serafina.

R.A.

*Winding the Skein.

R.A.

A Study.

R.A.

*Portrait of Miss Ruth Stewart Hodgson.

G.G.

Study of a Girl's Head.

G.G.

Sierra: Elviza in the distance, Granada.

S.S.

The Sierra Alhama, Granada.

S.S.

1879.

Biondina.

R.A.

Catarina.

R.A.

*Elijah in the Wilderness. (Paris, 1878.)

R.A.

Portrait of Signor G. Costa.

R.A.

Amarilla.

R.A.

A Study.

R.A.

Portrait of the Countess Brownlow.

R.A.

*Neruccia.

R.A.

A Study.

S.S.

The Carraca Hills.

S.S.

A Street in Lerici.

S.S.

Via Bianca, Capri.

G.G.

Archway in Algiers.

G.G.

Ruins of a Mosque, Damascus.

G.G.

Study of a Donkey.

G.G.

On the Terrace, Capri.

G.G.

Sketch Near Damascus.

G.G.

View in Granada.

G.G.

Study of a Donkey, Egypt.

G.G.

Study of a Head.
G.G.
Nicandra.
G.G.

1880.
*Sister's Kiss.
R.A.
*Iostephane.
R.A.
The Light of the Harem.
R.A.
Psamathe.
R.A.
*The Nymph of the Dargle (Crenaia).
R.A.
Rubinella.
G.G.
The Pozzo Corner, Venice. Winter Exhibition.
G.G.
Jack and his Cider Can. Winter Exhibition.
G.G.
The Painter's Honeymoon. Winter Exhibition.
G.G.
Winding of the Skein (with sketch). Winter Exhibition.
G.G.
Head of Urbino. Winter Exhibition.
G.G.
Steps of the Bargello, Florence. Winter Exhibition.
G.G.
A Contrast. Winter Exhibition.
G.G.
Garden at Capri. Winter Exhibition.
G.G.
Twenty-Nine Studies of Heads, Flowers, and Draperies.

Winter Exhibition.
G.G.

1881.
Elisha Raising the Son of the Shunamite. (Guildhall, 1895.)
R.A.
Portrait of the Painter. [19]
R.A.
*Idyll.
R.A.
*Portrait of Mrs. Stephen Ralli.
R.A.
*Whispers.
R.A.
Viola.
R.A.
*Bianca.
R.A.
Portrait of Mrs. Algernon Sartoris.
G.G.

1882.
*Day-dreams.
R.A.
Wedded.
R.A.
Phryne at Eleusis. (Melbourne, 1888.)
R.A.
Antigone. R.A.
"And the sea gave up the dead which were in it." *Rev.* xx. 13.
(Design for a portion of a decoration in St. Paul's.)
R.A.
Melittion.
R.A.
*Portrait of Mrs. Mocatta.

Zeyra.
G.G.

1883.
The Dance: decorative frieze for a drawing-room in a private house.
R.A.
*Vestal.
R.A.
*Kittens.
R.A.
Memories.
R.A.
*Portrait of Miss Nina Joachim.

1884.
*Letty.
R.A.
*Cymon and Iphigenia.
R.A.
A Nap.
R.A.
Sun Gleams.
R.A.

1885.
"... Serenely wandering in a trance Of sober Thought."
R.A.
Portrait of the Lady Sybil Primrose.
R.A.
*Portrait of Mrs. A. Hichens.
R.A.
Music: a frieze.
R.A.
Phœbe. (Manchester, 1887.)

R.A.
A Study.
G.G.
Tombs of Muslim Saints.
S.S.
Mountains near Ronda Puerta de los Vientos.
S.S.

1886.
Painted Decoration for the Ceiling of a Music-room. [20]
R.A.
Gulnihal.
R.A.
*The Sluggard. Statue, bronze.
R.A.
*Needless Alarms. Statuette.
R.A.
1887.
*The Jealousy of Simætha, the Sorceress.
R.A.
*The Last Watch of Hero.

"With aching heart she scanned the sea-face dim.
....

Lo! at the turret's foot his body lay,
Rolled on the stones, and washed with breaking spray."
Hero and Leander: Musæus (translated by Edwin Arnold).

R.A.
[Picture of A Little Girl with golden hair and pale blue eyes.]

"Yellow and pale as ripened corn
Which Autumn's kiss frees – grain from sheath –
Such was her hair, while her eyes beneath,
Showed Spring's faint violets freshly born."

Robert Browning.

*Design for the reverse of the Jubilee Medallion. (*Executed for Her Majesty's Government.*)

Empire, enthroned in the centre, rests her right hand on the sword of Justice, and holds in her left the symbol of victorious rule. At her feet, on one side, Commerce proffers wealth, on the other a winged figure holds emblems of Electricity and Steam-power. Flanking the throne to the right of the spectator are Agriculture and Industry – on the opposite side, Science, Literature, and the Arts. Above, interlocking wreaths, held by winged genii representing respectively the years 1837 and 1887, inclose the initials, V.R.I.

R.A.

1888.
*Captive Andromache.

"… Some standing by,
Marking thy tears fall, shall say, 'This is she,
The wife of that same Hector that fought best
Of all the Trojans, when all fought for Troy.'"
Iliad, VI. (E. B. Browning's translation.)

R.A.
*Portrait of Amy, Lady Coleridge. (S.P.P., 1891.)
R.A.
*Portraits of the Misses Stewart Hodgson.
Four Studies.
R.W.S.
Five Studies.
S.S.

1889.
*Sibyl.
R.A.

*Invocation.
R.A.
Elegy.
R.A.
Greek Girls playing at Ball.
R.A.
*Portrait of Mrs. Francis A. Lucas.
R.A.

1890.
Solitude.
R.A.
*The Bath of Psyche. [21]
R.A.
*Tragic Poetess.
R.A.
*The Arab Hall. (Guildhall, 1890.)
R.A.

1891.
*Perseus and Andromeda.
R.A.
*Portrait of A. B. Freeman-Mitford, Esq., C.B.
R.A.
*Return of Persephone.
R.A.
Athlete Struggling with a Python – group, marble.
R.A.

1892.
*"And the sea gave up the dead which were in it." (Circular)
R.A.
At the Fountain.
R.A.
*The Garden of the Hesperides. (Circular) (Chicago, 1893;

Guildhall, 1895.)
R.A.
Bacchante.
R.A.
*Clytie.
R.A.
Phryne at the Bath.
S.S.
Malin Head, Donegal.
S.S.
St. Mark's, Venice.
S.S.
Interior of St. Mark's, Venice.
S.S.
The Doorway, North Aisle, Venice.
S.S.
Rizpah (the small study in oils).
S.S.

1893.
*Farewell!
R.A.
*Hit!
R.A.
*Atalanta..)
R.A.
Rizpah.
R.A.
*Corinna of Tanagra.
R.A.
The Frigidarium.
R.A.

1894.
*The Spirit of the Summit.

R.A.

*The Bracelet.

R.A.

*Fatidica.

R.A.

*Summer Slumber.

R.A.

At the Window.

R.A.

Wide Wondering Eyes.

Manchester.

The Roman Campagna, Monte Soracte in the Distance.

S.S.

The Acropolis of Lindos.

S.S.

Fiume Morto, Gombo, Pisa.

S.S.

Gibraltar from San Rocque.

S.S.

1895.

Lachrymæ.

R.A.

The Maid with the Yellow Hair.

R.A.

*"'Twixt Hope and Fear."

R.A.

*Flaming June.

R.A.

Listener.

R.A.

A Study.

R.A.

Phœnicians Bartering With Britons.

Royal Exchange.

Boy with Pomegranate.
Grafton Gallery.
Miss Dene.
Aqua Certosa, Rome.
S.S.
Chain of Hills seen from Ronda.
S.S.
Rocks, Malin Head, Donegal.
S.S.
Tlemçen, Algeria.
S.S.

1896.
*Clytie.
R.A.
Candida.
Antwerp, 1896.
*The Vestal. Unfinished.
*A Bacchante.
*The Fair Persian. Unfinished.

APPENDIX II

The studies in oil, chiefly landscape, of quite small size, few of which had been exhibited, were sold, with the remaining works of the artist, by Messrs. Christie, Manson and Woods on July 11th, 13th, and 14th, 1896, when the prices realized, from 50 to 100 guineas each for the best, were in excess of those the most sympathetic admirer of Lord Leighton's singular power as a landscape-painter had dared to expect. For convenience of future reference, the list of these as they appear in the sale catalogue may be worth the space it occupies; the numbers denote the "lot."

1.Head of a Girl.
and Head of a Boy.
2. A Study of Houses, Venice.
3. The Coast of Asia Minor, from Rhodes.
4. A Street Scene.
5. Houses at Capri.
6. The Coast of Asia Minor, from Rhodes.
7. A Garden Scene.
8. A Fortress, Egypt.
9. Tombs of Muslim Saints at Assouan, First Cataract. R.S.B.A., 1895.
10. A Bay, Asia Minor, from Rhodes.
11. The Bay of Lindos.

12. In the Campagna, Italy.

13. A Town, Capri.

14. Mountains near Ronda Puerta de los Vientos. R.S.B.A., 1895.

15. A View in the Campagna.

16. A Covered Street in Algiers.

17. A Doorway, Algiers.

18. Head of a Girl.

19. Head of a Man.

20. Head of a Girl.

21. Head of a Girl.

22. Street in Algiers.

23. St. Mark's, Venice. R.S.B.A., 1892.

24. Interior of St. Mark's, Venice. R.S.B.A., 1892.

25. The Doorway, North Aisle, St. Mark's, Venice. R.S.B.A., 1892.

26. A Bay Scene, Isle of Rhodes.

27. A View on the Coast, Lindos.

28. Denderah.

29. The Roman Campagna, Monte Soracte in the Distance. R.S.B.A., 1894.

30. A Study in the Campagna.

31. Aqua Certosa, Rome.

32. A View of the Town of Lindos.

33. The Acropolis of Lindos, where stood the Temple of Athena Pallas. R.S.B.A., 1894.

34. A Study in the Campagna, with Monte Soracte.

35. Study of a Man's Head.

36. An Arab's Head.

37. A Sheik.

38. An Arab.

39. Head of an Old Lady.

40. A Turkish Boatman.

41. Fiume Morto, Gombo, Pisa. R.S.B.A., 1894.

42. The Citadel, Cairo.

43. A View in Damascus.

44. A View in Capri.

45. Bocca d'Arno.

46. The City of Tombs, Assiout, Egypt. R.S.B.A. [1871?].

47. Buildings, Siout, Egypt.

48. A Mountainous Landscape, Spain.

49. A Street Scene, Capri.

50. A Coast Scene, Isle of Wight.

51. Barren Land.

52. A Town in Spain.

53. Bosco Sacro, Campagna.

54. Villa Malta, Rome.

55. The Rocks of the Sirens, Capri.

56. A View in Spain.

57. A Valley, Spain.

58. On the Coast, Isle of Wight.

59. Garden at Generalife, Granada.

60. The Baths at Caracalla.

61. A House, Capri.

62. In St. Mark's, Venice.

63. The Staircase of a House, Capri.

64. The Garden of a House, Capri.

65. Study of a Male Figure carrying a Pitcher.

66. Head of a Girl.

67. The Coast of Asia Minor, from Rhodes.

68. Chain of Hills seen from Ronda. R.S.B.A., 1893.

69. The Coast of Asia Minor. (Study for the background of *Perseus*.)

70. A Pool, Findhorn River, N.B. (Study for the background of *Solitude*.)

71. A Lane. (Study of rocks for *Solitude*.)

72. A Woman seated, in a landscape. (Study for *Simætha the Sorceress*.)

73. Taormina, Sicily. (Sketch for background of *Wedded*.)

74. A Pool on the Findhorn River, Forres, N.B. (Study for the

background of *Solitude*.)

75. Taormina, Sicily. (Study for the background of *Wedded*.)

76. Interior of a House at Lindos. (Study for the picture of *Cleoboulos*.)

77. Study of a Woman's Head. Capri, moonlight. (Study for the effect in *Clytemnestra*.)

78. Buildings, Capri, Moonlight. (A study for the same.)

79. An Allegorical Design for a Mural Decoration.

80. Head of a Lady and Gentleman of the Fifteenth Century. (16 x 14? in.) (Painted in 1853.)

81. Head of a Lady. White on brown ground.

82. A Study from Velasquez.

[83 to 117 *were larger works, mainly studies for completed pictures or the pictures themselves*.]

118. A Landscape.
and Study of Sky at Malinmore.
and Study.

119. A Rocky Coast, Malinmore, Donegal.

120. A Mountainous Landscape.

121. A View in Scotland.

122. A Landscape, Italy.

123. Fishing Boats on the Coast, Capri.

124. A Village on a Hill, Capri.

125. A Scene in the Desert.

126. The Coast of Greece.

127. Head of a Man.

128. A Scotch Lake.

129. Near Kynance Cove.

130. Carrara Mountains.

131. A View in Algiers.

132. Tlemçen, Algeria. R.S.B.A., 1895.

133. The Damascus Gate, Jerusalem.

134. The Erictheum (*sic*).

135. A Street in Lerici, near where Shelley was drowned.
136. Study of Trees.
and A Landscape.
137. Head of a Gondolier.
and Irish Peasant Girl.
138. Head of an Italian Peasant.
139. A Common.
and Landscape, with Cottages.
140. A Rocky Coast, Kynance.
141. Granite Boulders, Forres, N.B.
142. A Sunny Cornfield.
143. A Courtyard, Tangiers.
144. A Courtyard, Tangiers.
145. A Sketch of Albano.
146. A Coast Scene, Ireland.
147. A Scotch Scene.
148. A Study of Rocks.
149. The Steeple Rock, Kynance Cove.
150. A Sandy Bay, Ireland.
151. Kynance Cove.
152. Holy Island. Bamborough in the distance.
153. A Coast Scene, Ischia.
154. Glen Columbkill, Ireland.
155. A Moorish Archway, Tangiers.
156. Perugia.
157. A Rocky Coast, Malinmore.
158. Malin Head, Donegal. R.S.B.A., 1894.
159. Gibraltar, from San Rocque. R.S.B.A., 1895.
160. A Bay Scene, Spain.
161. A Sketch in Bedfordshire.
162. A Landscape, Ronda.
163. A Spanish Town.
164. The Baths of Caracalla.
165. The Street of the Knights, Rhodes.
166. The Coast of Asia Minor, seen from Rhodes.

167. Longsor.

168. A Mountain Scene, with Temple and Figure, Egypt.

169. A Study on the Coast of Ireland.

170. A River Scene, Scotland.

171. Mickleour, Scotland.

172. A Sea Piece.

173. The Coast of Asia Minor.

174. On the Nile.

and A View in Spain.

175. A Temple on the Nile.

and Spanish View.

176. Malinmore, Donegal.

177. The Bay of Cadiz, Moonlight, and Palazzo Rezzonico.

178. A View of Athens.

179. Scotch Mountains: Sunset.

and A Coast Scene, Rhodes.

180. Vittoria. R.S.B.A., 1873.

181. A Classical Head. (Monochrome.)

and Head of a Man.

182. A Study of Pine Trees.

183. A Village on a Hill.

184. A Ruined Mosque at Broussa.

185. A Woody Bank.

186. Ruins of a Moorish Arch, Spain.

187. A View in Italy, with a Cornfield.

188. (This number is omitted in the sale catalogue.)

189. Mimbar of the Great Mosque at Damascus.

190. Rocks, Capri.

and A Fortress, Spain.

191. Landscape, Scotland.

and Landscape, Scotland.

192. The Red Mountains, Desert, Egypt.

193. Sketch near Cairo.

194. A Fountain in the Court-yard of a Jew's House, Spain.

195. A House in Tangiers. Mansion House, 1882.

196. A Street Scene, Cairo.

197. A Moorish Street.

198. A Study of Rocks, Scotland.

199. The Garden of the House of the Man who built the Alhambra.

200. A Spanish Donkey.

201. A Donkey and Arab Driver.

202. Mena Donkey.

203. A Study of Hills.

204. The Temple of Phylæ.

205. Damascus: Night.

206. A Mountainous Landscape, with a Cavern.

207. A Wood Scene.

208. Head of an Italian Girl.

209. The Dungeons of a Castle.

210. A Castle Keep.

211. Entrance to a House, Capri.

212. A Coast Scene, Ireland: Storm effort (*sic*).

213. Longsor.

214. The Nile at Thebes.

215. A View on the Campagna.

216. A Mountainous Landscape, Scotland.

217. Capri by Night.

218. A Fortress on the Campagna.

219. A Landscape, with Sand Hills.

220. A Wood Scene.

221. Near Denderah.

222. A Landscape.

223. Athens, with the Genoese Tower, Pnyx in the foreground.

224. A Landscape, Cairo.

225. On the Nile.

226. Pasture, Egypt.

227. Red Mountains Desert, Egypt.

228. An Egyptian Village.

229. The Island of Ægina.

230. Thebes.

231. The Coast of Ægina, Pnyx in the foreground.

232. Buildings on the Coast, Island of Rhodes.

233. Assouan, Egypt.

234. A Vineyard, Capri.

235. The Temple of Phylæ, looking up the Nile.

236. The Nile at Esueh.

237. The Cathedral, Capri.

238. A Square in Cadiz.

239. On the Nile.

240. In the Nile Valley.

241. A View across the Nile.

242. A Woody Hill Side.

243. Rocks of the Sirens Capri.

244. A Farm.

There were also copies made by Leighton himself of *Peace and War* after Rubens, the *Massacre of the Innocents*, after Bonifazio, *A Martyrdom*, and the *Last Supper*, after Veronese.

The huge collection of studies, mainly in chalk upon brown paper, made by Lord Leighton, were nearly all preserved; two hundred and forty of these were exhibited by the Fine Art Society, who bought the whole collection, and afterwards published a volume containing forty reproduced in facsimile.

FOOTNOTES

1. See pages 119-120.

2. Letter to William Allingham, May 10th, 1861.

3. "Athenæum," April, 1864.

4. The original title of this picture was *Eastern Slinger scaring Birds in Harvest-time: Moonrise.*

5. This picture was re-sold at Christie's in 1892 for 3,750 guineas.

6. Sometimes entitled *An Athlete strangling a Python.*

7. At page 82.

8. Engraved in the "Magazine of Art," March, 1896.

9. "Current Art" ("Magazine of Art," May, 1889).

10. "The Studio," vol. iii.

11. Reproductions not included in this book.

12. "Letters of Dante Gabriel Rossetti to William Allingham," by George Birkbeck Hill, D.C.L., LL.D. London, T. Fisher Unwin, 1897.

13. "La Peinture Anglaise Contemporaine" (Paris, Hachette, 1895).

14. "Magazine of Art," March, 1896, p. 197.

15. The asterisk denotes works exhibited at the Winter Exhibition of the Royal Academy of Arts, 1897.

16. R.A., Royal Academy; G.G., Grosvenor Gallery; R.W.S., Royal Society of Painters in Water-Colours; S.S., Royal Society of

British Artists, Suffolk Street; D.G., Dudley Gallery; S.P.P., Society of Portrait Painters.

17. Exhibited in the Roman Section, by some blunder of the Committee; the picture having been painted in Rome.

18. Purchased for £2,000 by the President and Council of the Royal Academy, under the terms of the Chantrey Bequest.

19. Painted by invitation for the Collection of Portraits of Artists painted by themselves in the Uffizi Gallery, Florence.

20. Painted for the house of Mr. Murquand, New York.

21. Purchased for 1,000 guineas by the President and Council of the Royal Academy, under the terms of the Chantrey Bequest.

CRESCENT MOON PUBLISHING

web: www.crmoon.com e-mail: cresmopub@yahoo.co.uk

ARTS, PAINTING, SCULPTURE

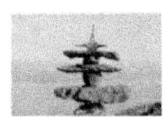
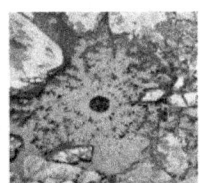
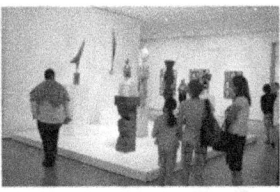
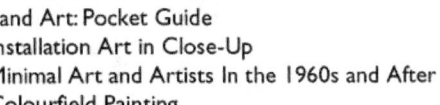
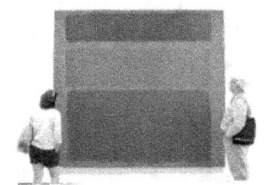
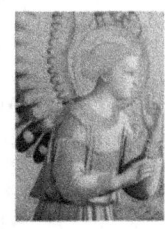

The Art of Andy Goldsworthy
Andy Goldsworthy: Touching Nature
Andy Goldsworthy in Close-Up
Andy Goldsworthy: Pocket Guide
Andy Goldsworthy In America
Land Art: A Complete Guide
The Art of Richard Long
Richard Long: Pocket Guide
Land Art In the UK
Land Art in Close-Up
Land Art In the U.S.A.
Land Art: Pocket Guide
Installation Art in Close-Up
Minimal Art and Artists In the 1960s and After
Colourfield Painting
Land Art DVD, TV documentary
Andy Goldsworthy DVD, TV documentary
The Erotic Object: Sexuality in Sculpture From Prehistory to the Present Day
Sex in Art: Pornography and Pleasure in Painting and Sculpture
Postwar Art
Sacred Gardens: The Garden in Myth, Religion and Art
Glorification: Religious Abstraction in Renaissance and 20th Century Art
Early Netherlandish Painting
Leonardo da Vinci
Piero della Francesca
Giovanni Bellini
Fra Angelico: Art and Religion in the Renaissance
Mark Rothko: The Art of Transcendence
Frank Stella: American Abstract Artist
Jasper Johns
Brice Marden
Alison Wilding: The Embrace of Sculpture
Vincent van Gogh: Visionary Landscapes
Eric Gill: Nuptials of God
Constantin Brancusi: Sculpting the Essence of Things
Max Beckmann
Caravaggio
Gustave Moreau
Egon Schiele: Sex and Death In Purple Stockings
Delizioso Fotografico Fervore: Works In Process 1
Sacro Cuore: Works In Process 2
The Light Eternal: J.M.W. Turner
The Madonna Glorified: Karen Arthurs

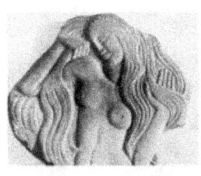
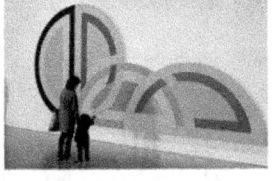
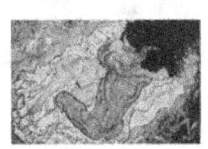
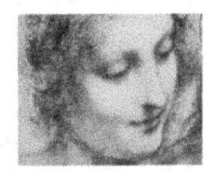
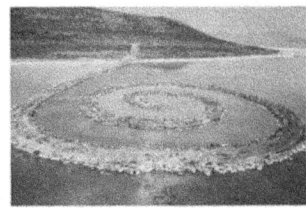

LITERATURE

J.R.R. Tolkien: The Books, The Films, The Whole Cultural Phenomenon
J.R.R. Tolkien: Pocket Guide
Tolkien's Heroic Quest
The *Earthsea* Books of Ursula Le Guin
Beauties, Beasts and Enchantment: Classic French Fairy Tales
German Popular Stories by the Brothers Grimm
Philip Pullman and *His Dark Materials*
Sexing Hardy: Thomas Hardy and Feminism
Thomas Hardy's *Tess of the d'Urbervilles*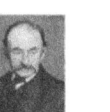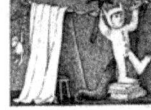
Thomas Hardy's *Jude the Obscure*
Thomas Hardy: The Tragic Novels
Love and Tragedy: Thomas Hardy
The Poetry of Landscape in Hardy
Wessex Revisited: Thomas Hardy and John Cowper Powys
Wolfgang Iser: Essays and Interviews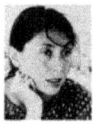
Petrarch, Dante and the Troubadours
Maurice Sendak and the Art of Children's Book Illustration
Andrea Dworkin
Cixous, Irigaray, Kristeva: The *Jouissance* of French Feminism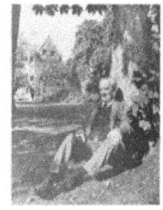
Julia Kristeva: Art, Love, Melancholy, Philosophy, Semiotics and Psychoanalysis
Hélène Cixous I Love You: The *Jouissance* of Writing
Luce Irigaray: Lips, Kissing, and the Politics of Sexual Difference
Peter Redgrove: Here Comes the Flood
Peter Redgrove: Sex-Magic-Poetry-Cornwall
Lawrence Durrell: Between Love and Death, East and West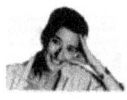
Love, Culture & Poetry: Lawrence Durrell
Cavafy: Anatomy of a Soul
German Romantic Poetry: Goethe, Novalis, Heine, Hölderlin
Feminism and Shakespeare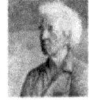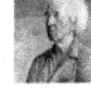
Shakespeare: Love, Poetry & Magic
The Passion of D.H. Lawrence
D.H. Lawrence: Symbolic Landscapes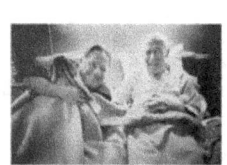
D.H. Lawrence: Infinite Sensual Violence
Rimbaud: Arthur Rimbaud and the Magic of Poetry
The Ecstasies of John Cowper Powys
Sensualism and Mythology: The Wessex Novels of John Cowper Powys
Amorous Life: John Cowper Powys and the Manifestation of Affectivity (H.W. Fawkner)
Postmodern Powys: New Essays on John Cowper Powys (Joe Boulter)
Rethinking Powys: Critical Essays on John Cowper Powys
Paul Bowles & Bernardo Bertolucci
Rainer Maria Rilke
Joseph Conrad: *Heart of Darkness*
In the Dim Void: Samuel Beckett
Samuel Beckett Goes into the Silence
André Gide: Fiction and Fervour
Jackie Collins and the Blockbuster Novel
Blinded By Her Light: The Love-Poetry of Robert Graves
The Passion of Colours: Travels In Mediterranean Lands
Poetic Forms

POETRY

Ursula Le Guin: Walking In Cornwall
Peter Redgrove: Here Comes The Flood
Peter Redgrove: Sex-Magic-Poetry-Cornwall
Dante: Selections From the Vita Nuova
Petrarch, Dante and the Troubadours
William Shakespeare: Sonnets
William Shakespeare: Complete Poems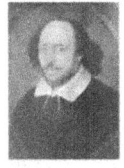
Blinded By Her Light: The Love-Poetry of Robert Graves
Emily Dickinson: Selected Poems
Emily Brontë: Poems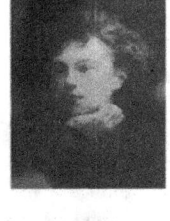
Thomas Hardy: Selected Poems
Percy Bysshe Shelley: Poems
John Keats: Selected Poems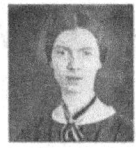
Joh n Keats: Poems of 1820
D.H. Lawrence: Selected Poems
Edmund Spenser: Poems
Edmund Spenser: Amoretti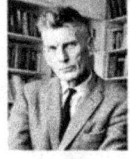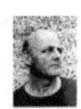
John Donne: Poems
Henry Vaughan: Poems
Sir Thomas Wyatt: Poems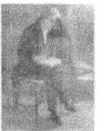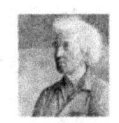
Robert Herrick: Selected Poems
Rilke: Space, Essence and Angels in the Poetry of Rainer Maria Rilke
Rainer Maria Rilke: Selected Poems
Friedrich Hölderlin: Selected Poems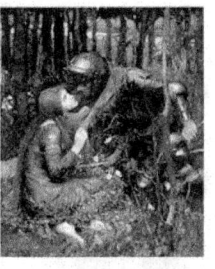
Arseny Tarkovsky: Selected Poems
Arthur Rimbaud: Selected Poems
Arthur Rimbaud: A Season in Hell
Arthur Rimbaud and the Magic of Poetry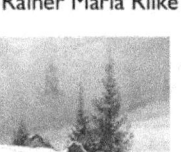
Novalis: Hymns To the Night
German Romantic Poetry
Paul Verlaine: Selected Poems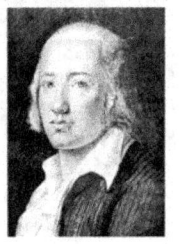
Elizaethan Sonnet Cycles
D.J. Enright: By-Blows
Jeremy Reed: Brigitte's Blue Heart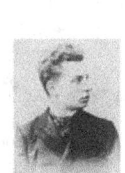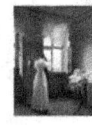
Jeremy Reed: Claudia Schiffer's Red Shoes
Gorgeous Little Orpheus
Radiance: New Poems
Crescent Moon Book of Nature Poetry
Crescent Moon Book of Love Poetry
Crescent Moon Book of Mystical Poetry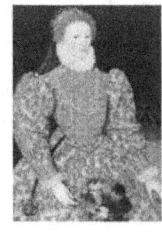
Crescent Moon Book of Elizabethan Love Poetry
Crescent Moon Book of Metaphysical Poetry
Crescent Moon Book of Romantic Poetry
Pagan America: New American Poetry

MEDIA, CINEMA, FEMINISM and CULTURAL STUDIES

J.R.R. Tolkien: The Books, The Films, The Whole Cultural Phenomenon
J.R.R. Tolkien: Pocket Guide
The *Lord of the Rings* Movies: Pocket Guide
The Cinema of Hayao Miyazaki
Hayao Miyazaki: *Princess Mononoke*: Pocket Movie Guide
Hayao Miyazaki: *Spirited Away*: Pocket Movie Guide
Tim Burton : Hallowe'en For Hollywood
Ken Russell
Ken Russell: *Tommy*: Pocket Movie Guide
The Ghost Dance: The Origins of Religion
The Peyote Cult

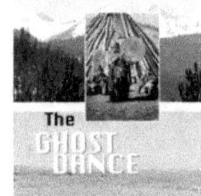

Cixous, Irigaray, Kristeva: The *Jouissance* of French Feminism
Julia Kristeva: Art, Love, Melancholy, Philosophy, Semiotics and Psychoanalysis
Luce Irigaray: Lips, Kissing, and the Politics of Sexual Difference
Hélene Cixous I Love You: The *Jouissance* of Writing
Andrea Dworkin
'Cosmo Woman': The World of Women's Magazines
Women in Pop Music
HomeGround: The Kate Bush Anthology
Discovering the Goddess (Geoffrey Ashe)
The Poetry of Cinema
The Sacred Cinema of Andrei Tarkovsky
Andrei Tarkovsky: Pocket Guide
Andrei Tarkovsky: *Mirror*: Pocket Movie Guide
Andrei Tarkovsky: *The Sacrifice*: Pocket Movie Guide
Walerian Borowczyk: Cinema of Erotic Dreams
Jean-Luc Godard: The Passion of Cinema
Jean-Luc Godard: *Hail Mary*: Pocket Movie Guide
Jean-Luc Godard: *Contempt*: Pocket Movie Guide
Jean-Luc Godard: *Pierrot le Fou*: Pocket Movie Guide
John Hughes and Eighties Cinema
Ferris Bueller's Day Off: Pocket Movie Guide
Jean-Luc Godard: Pocket Guide
The Cinema of Richard Linklater
Liv Tyler: Star In Ascendance
Blade Runner and the Films of Philip K. Dick
Paul Bowles and Bernardo Bertolucci
Media Hell: Radio, TV and the Press
An Open Letter to the BBC
Detonation Britain: Nuclear War in the UK
Feminism and Shakespeare
Wild Zones: Pornography, Art and Feminism
Sex in Art: Pornography and Pleasure in Painting and Sculpture
Sexing Hardy: Thomas Hardy and Feminism

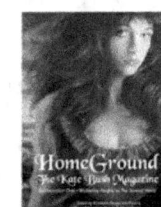

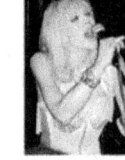

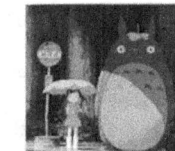

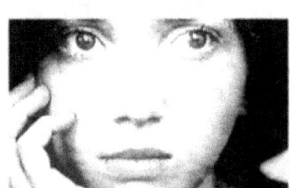

The Light Eternal is a model monograph, an exemplary job. The subject matter of the book is beautifully
organised and dead on beam. (Lawrence Durrell)
It is amazing for me to see my work treated with such passion and respect. (Andrea Dworkin)

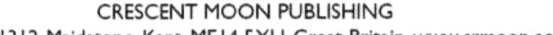

CRESCENT MOON PUBLISHING
P.O. Box 1312, Maidstone, Kent, ME14 5XU, Great Britain. www.crmoon.com

cresmopub@yahoo.co.uk   www.crescentmoon.org.uk